How I Got Hurt

NOTE: It Could Be Because I'm Stupid

By Larry Buenafe

Foreword

They say that confession is good for the soul. If that's true, I should have one of the healthier souls around after all that's to come in this confession-fest. Why should you care about all this? No good reason, really, aside from reading some amusing, cringe-worthy stories, after which you can hopefully feel better about yourself: "I may have done some crappy things in my life but at least I'm not stupid enough to do *that*." So, in a way I suppose this could be seen as a public service; an attempt to buoy your self-esteem by inviting comparisons in which you will invariably come out the winner. *You're welcome*. Here's a word, and definition, that will come in handy as you read on:

Schadenfreude

Here's how Miriam-Webster defines it:

Enjoyment obtained from the troubles of others

I have heard that bit of enjoyment at the misfortunes of others can be a sure way to make you feel better about yourself. It's a self-affirming boost, especially if you feel the other person deserves the misfortune. Once again, *you're welcome*.

So how did all this idiocy come about? Could it be...

Hubris, maybe?

Here's how the Urban Dictionary describes it:

From the Greek word of the same spelling, the concept of overweaning pride, or expectations that far exceed the scope of one's being.

I'm not sure what overweaning means, so let's keep looking...

How about plain old **recklessness**?

From the New Thesaurus:

The trait of giving little thought to danger.

That's pretty close, but what about...

Stupidity? Surely not...

From Miriam-Webster:

...the state of being foolish or unintelligent: the condition of being stupid

Uh-oh...better define **stupid**...

Also, from Miriam-Webster:

Not intelligent; having or showing a lack of ability to learn and understand things; not sensible or logical

Expectations that far exceed the scope of one's being; giving little thought to danger; the state of being foolish or unintelligent; not sensible or logical. These are some of the reasons I got hurt. It's tempting to say that I acquired all these injuries, both physical and emotional, just so that I would have this array of amusing anecdotes to pass on. You know, like a kidney stone. I've passed a few of those on, too. Of course, reality is a bit more complex and nuanced than that.

There are lots of folks who have been hurt worse than me, and I'm not trying to say that there was some kind of nobility to my injuries. In fact, if anything, I'd say it's the opposite of that. Also, don't assume that this is just some hyper-verbal version of the MTV show "Jack Ass". Unlike those fellows, I wasn't attempting to injure myself (or at least not consciously), and I sure wasn't attempting to entertain anyone, except maybe myself (ditto). However, very much like them, many of my calamities were at least partially hormone-induced; it's worth noting that the very thing that provides for the survival of the species also reduces us, at our most hormone-florid moments, to a primitive version of our species. Well, we only have to look at any area of popular culture to see that we will do almost anything for a boner.

As anyone who has had, or has been around, a boy, which statistically probably includes a lot of us knows, boys, or perhaps males in general, are rather prone to hazardous behavior. Sort of like the precarious number of commas included in that last sentence—*very* hazardous sentence structure. I know there are some of you who will say, "Oh yeah, you should see my (insert daughter, granddaughter, sister, niece, cousin, friend, girlfriend, female farm animal, etc. here)—she's *craaaazy*." Yes, of course, there are exceptions in both (or should I say all) genders and orientations, but let's deal with reality on reality's terms, and agree that, *in general*, males are more compelled by the particular mix of chemicals flowing through their bodies to engage in activities that could lead to harm, damage, and grievance.

There are many ways to harm oneself, and not all include physical harm, at least not initially. A particular mix of upbringing, experiences, and genetics can lead to some very specific self-injurious behaviors—think anorexia for an explicit example. This kind of behavior is not possible in an undamaged mind; logically we know we must eat to continue to survive, and most anorexics don't really want to kill themselves, and yet their behavior will lead there if left unchecked. It's unlikely that these folks aspired to anorexia as youngsters, and yet somehow their self-image is so loathsome that they attempt, in a quantifiable way, to cause themselves to disappear. So, if they know their behavior may lead to their death, but they aren't attempting to kill themselves, why would anyone do it? And more crucially, how can it be prevented? When I have the answer to that second question, I'll let you know from my private island in the Bahamas, because I'll be able to charge a whale's buttload for it.

Of course, there are many other examples of behaviors that lead to self-harm that are not undertaken for that specific purpose, any number of which you can name for yourself; nevertheless, once they have their hooks into you in the form of the emotional and physical rewards they provide, they are very hard to extinguish. You may suspect by now that all this blather and twaddle is a way for me to let you in on my own little corner of instability, to which I can only say, 'well, no shit, Sherlock'. Oh, by the way, there will be a few "bad words" (or *malas palabras* for some of my friends here in central California) in the stories to come, such as the dreaded "S" word in the sentence you just read. In most cases I am simply quoting others, but on one or two occasions I uttered the expletive myself, but look, we're all adults here, right? If you read on, you'll get a glimpse into my own particular kind of illness; suck up all the chewy, delicious *schadenfreude-iness* you can stomach, and then stuff in a little more, because that's the American way.

All the stories included here are true, and as accurate as my memory can make them. It is possible here and there that some of the details got a little jumbled in the mists of time; if you read this and happen to recognize yourself in any of the stories, please don't write me and try to settle my hash by correcting me on some extraneous detail. Just read it and try to have a little fun for once in your life, why don't you? *Sheesh!*

I will change names, grudgingly; some of the people I will mention had (and have) awesome names, and some of them deserve to have their real names included because they should be publicly shamed for their dreadful behavior. Some would get a little thrill out of having their real name herein; for that reason, I definitely will not be including them.

Finally, I struggled a little with how to organize these stories. I considered a number of ways, including some variation on the seven deadly sins (which, if spelled with a Z at the end, would be a sweet name for a heavy metal band—maybe "7 Dedlee Sinz"), but in the end, like water rolling downhill, I settled for the easiest method, which will be a vaguely chronological ordering (I believe there may be a Ska band by the name of Vaguely Chronological, by the way).

The Great Lawnmower Caper

I remember when John F. Kennedy was assassinated. I know, 'Dude, you're *old*'. Whatever. I really only knew it through my mother's reaction; I saw her in the back yard of our sad little house on Cain Street, right on the corner of Crappy and Crappier. She was crying, really sobbing, and I had no idea why. I had only just turned six, so I really couldn't fathom such adult matters at that time, but I could definitely feel the pain of all the adults. It was a menacing time to grow up; the existential, yet as far as we knew very real, threat of atomic war loomed over us like the guillotine over Marie Antoinette, and it was all made worse by the depressing realization, even at six years old, that there was literally nothing we could do to prevent it or protect ourselves if it came.

So, what did the government do to provide the illusion of protection for us small children? They had us *perform drills to protect ourselves in the event of a nuclear holocaust, at school.* If they had started with the mass terrorization of children as their goal, they could not have devised a better plan. Here's how the drill would go: our teacher, Mrs. Oakes (who was a *bitch* who, for some unknown reason, hated me—she described me, in my report card, as *lazy and disruptive*, not that I am bitter about it or anything) would say to the class, "Alright, children, we will soon be performing a disaster drill. When the bell rings repeatedly, you will get under your desk. This will protect you in the case of a nuclear attack." The first thing we had to do was figure out what "repeatedly" meant, followed immediately by, "I don't think my desk can stop an atomic bomb." You will of course remember school desks—a piece of particle board with a faux wood sheathing, approximately three feet by two feet, a plastic seat and seat back, and some tubular metal legs—perfect for protection from atomic fallout. Still, like good little soldiers, we all performed our task (though I remember Artie Pinkler falling asleep under his desk—clearly, he didn't tie into the zeitgeist-y angst as much as the rest of us). For me, already a fearful, clingy child, the sense of dread and impending doom was a lot to bear.

We lived in a small tract house in an area that would now be described as either somewhat or extremely ghettoesque, depending on your frame of reference. It was painted one of those vague, beige-ish tract house colors on the stucco outside, and my dad put in some cheap wood paneling on one wall of the living room to class the place up. He didn't cut it quite right, though, and there were some rips here and there on the edges. I really didn't realize at the time that it was that bad, but going back and looking at it now, surrounded by section-8 apartments, dirty diapers and beer bottles filling the gutters, people shuffling around in tattered tank tops with pictures of Sponge Bob, with his name written in Spanish (*Esponja Roberto*!), we were circling the toilet and on our way down. I had three siblings at the time (a fourth came along much later—that is a story unto itself), and each of us were a year apart; one older brother and two younger sisters (my parents were clearly "getting busy" during those years). Typical of second children, I learned to keep my mouth shut, not attract attention (at least from my dad), and if I wanted to do anything, to do it quietly.

We really were quite poor in those days, although that's not something you are acutely aware of as a young child; it was more a feeling of pressure and desperation than something tangible at the time. My father was decidedly blue-collar, working as a welder for a nearby feed mill; I just remember him as being gone all the time, and when he was home, he was tired and always on the verge of angry. I really felt the desperation from my mother—she just seemed overwhelmed and depressed most of the time (hey, I thought this book was supposed to be funny—I think I am getting ripped off here—oh wait, I'm writing it. Sorry, I'll get on it.)

So, now to the story. We had an old, hand-me-down push-mower (most of you have probably never seen one of these; it's a simple device with several long, twisted blades that rotate via the power of a person rather than a motor; it is a very labor-intensive way to mow a lawn, let me tell you). My dad was not good at keeping up the yardwork, and my mom eventually became disgusted and went outside to mow the front grass herself. She got about halfway through before getting exhausted, and she just left the mower in the front yard where she stopped. It makes me a little sad to think about it now; I think she was quite depressed and felt like a failure ('I can't even mow the lawn right!' Oh, wait, bring the funny, okay).

The next morning, which happened to be a Saturday, I walked out into the front yard to see an older kid who I vaguely recognized from the neighborhood walking away pulling the dilapidated push mower behind him. After a moment, I realized, "Hey, he's stealing our mower!" In retrospect, I suppose I may have thought that he was doing us a favor, as it probably would have forced my dad to go to garage sales until he found a "new" mower, one of the fancy ones with a motor on it. Nevertheless, I instead took chase, and the kid noticed, as he began to run, still pulling the mower behind him. When you pull, or push, one of these mowers the blades spin, and it is not easy to make them go fast, so I was able to catch up with him rather quickly; again, in retrospect I may have opted for a more casual approach, but that is not what I did. Instead, I urged my pudgy little legs to propel me at maximum velocity. I really don't know why he was running; he was twice my size and could have easily stopped me with a nice kick to the nads, or karate chop to the throat; you know, standard techniques for fending off little kids.

At any rate, as I approached, he was exiting the lawn and now had the mower in the gutter. I knew that once he got the mower into the street, he would be able to pull it faster and would be able to complete his nefarious task, so I put on a final burst of speed, then tripped headlong into the gutter, my arms splayed out in front of me.

Unfortunately, I was close enough to grab the mower with this final burst, and the middle finger on my left hand fell into the spinning blade of the mower, slicing off the end of the finger rather cleanly. I don't remember feeling anything initially; I looked down and saw the end of my finger on the ground, picked it up and stuck it back on the remainder of my finger. At this point, I think Biff, or whatever his name was, panicked; he released the push mower and ran away. I may have been in a little bit of shock, as I don't remember what happened next; somehow, I dragged the mower back into the yard and walked into the house to show mom what had happened. I don't remember going to the hospital, but one way or another the end of the finger got sown back on, where it remains today.

What is the moral of the story? Spend the money and buy a good mower; you won't regret it. Pay cheap and weep, friends, pay cheap and weep.

Man's Best Friend

When I was seven, my dad brought home a German shepherd puppy, and of course my siblings and I were overjoyed. As you may know, German shepherds are very protective of their humans and can be quite aggressive against other humans if not trained properly. Well, training of that kind was a bridge much too far for us—we couldn't train ourselves, much less a dog. Bobby, the German shepherd, grew large rather quickly, and he did what his instincts and centuries of breeding instructed him to do; he protected us at for all he was worth. This might sound like a good thing, but...

I can recall two separate incidents in which Bobby's instinct for protection led to his demise. The first involved my brother having a tussle with an older kid. In those days, after you finished riding around the neighborhood on your bike, you would just flop the bike down on the driveway and go inside, without a thought about someone trying to steal it. You would never do that these days, but the times were somewhat different. Similarly, my parents never locked the house or the car; they stubbornly persisted with this practice throughout their lives, refusing to believe that their neighbors would take advantage of them by stealing from them. Of course, times did change even though they did not; various items were ripped off over the years, although to be honest they didn't have a whole lot that anyone would want.

So, one afternoon, when my brother, who was eight at the time, came out of the house on Cain Street, he found an older kid walking away with his bike. He ran and grabbed the bike by the handlebars and tried to take it away from the would-be bike thief; Bobby the German

Shepherd, protector, guardian, dark knight, was in the back yard 15 feet away, and was literally going wild. In a moment of inspiration, my brother called for the dog, and that was all it took; he rammed into the fence head-first, knocking a board loose, ran up and latched on to the leg of the bike thief and attempted to remove it from his body. Well, the kid screamed, understandably, and attempted to run away, but Bobby was having none of it, and continued tearing at him until he was rescued by my mother. Nowadays we would be at the wrong end of a lawsuit, but in those days, folks would say "it serves him right", so Bobby escaped the gas chamber on that occasion. Unfortunately, not too much later, he sealed his own fate.

On the day in question, I made the unfortunate mistake of trying to take Bobby for a walk. I put him on a leash and took him out into the front yard; at that moment, a lady with two small children walked by on the street, and Bobby went into attack mode. I tried to hold him back, but he pulled me off my feet and dragged my fat little seven-year-old body across the road to get to the panicked pedestrians, and shortly after he was "taken to the country to live on a farm".

Now, to the real story. In the backyard of our sad little house on Cain Street, in the far corner where the fences came together, was a telephone pole. One of the sure signs of living in a bad part of town is having a telephone pole in your backyard. Next to the telephone pole was a gap in the fence about four inches wide, and on the other side of the fence was an open field. One day, not long after Bobby went to the country, I was in the backyard, and I noticed through the gap in the fence a dog that very much resembled Bobby approaching through the empty field. I loved Bobby; he was gentle and tolerant with me, and I had no reason to believe that a dog who looked similar would not behave in a similar manner. So, I stuck my pudgy little arm through the gap and called to the dog, so that I could pet it; it came close, then latched on to my bicep with its canines and attempted to pull me through the four-inch gap. I don't really know what happened next; I must have screamed or somehow got the dog to release me; maybe I didn't taste good, maybe the dog was trying to watch his cholesterol, I don't know. I ended up with large, dog-tooth-shaped scars on each side of my right bicep. In the intervening years I have tried to convince people that it is a bullet wound procured during a gang fight, but I can't pull it off.

The moral of the story? If you are contemplating buying a house and you find that there is a telephone pole in the backyard, keep looking; that's ghetto.

Hairy Goonafay, the Bacon Boy

As we have found, injury can come in many forms and can sometimes have a delayed impact, especially if the injury is emotional or psychological in nature. In this case, it is a bit of a stretch to call it an injury, since for me to experience the admittedly minor embarrassment and humiliation of the incident, I had to recount it, usually verbally but here committing it to the digital version of paper, in exchange for a snicker or guffaw or mildly amused "humpf!", so who is the victim? You decide, why do I have to do all the work here?

To set the scene, let me first say that, as an eight-year-old, like many of my peers, I was drawn like a moth to the sun when it was cartoon time on the three-channel TV with vice grips where the channel knob used to be, having long ago snapped off. There was a local show called Jimmy Weldon and Webster Webfoot, on during the school day so I normally missed it. Jimmy Weldon was a Ventriloquist, Webster Webfoot his anthropomorphic duck puppet. Sounds amazing so far, am I right? They would do a little skit, then show a cartoon or two, come on with another skit, then more cartoons, etc. So, here's the story:

On the day in question, I was home ill. Was I really ill? I don't know, might have been the I-hate-school flu, I'm not sure. At any rate, on this particular day I had somehow convinced my mom to allow me to stay home, a rare feat indeed, and was parked, immovable, in front of the TV as Jimmy Weldon and Webster Webfoot spun their cheesy magic. I lapped it up, focusing on every word, every movement. As luck would have it, or in my case the opposite of luck... surely there is a word for it besides simply "bad luck"... stand by... okay, I looked up antonyms for luck and the consensus is that the word is misfortune. I don't know, seems kind of awkward, but we'll go with it for now. So, I had the misfortune of hearing Jimmy Weldon say that the following day, he would be doing a performance at the grand opening of a supermarket just down the street from my school. How could I miss a live performance by Jimmy Weldon and the hilarious Webster Webfoot? The answer, of course, was *I could not.*

Needless to say, I had to go to school the next day or there was no way my mother would let me go to the big show, so I quickly recovered from my probably fake illness, and there I was after school, front and center, enthralled as only an eight-year-old could be in front of a middle-aged man with a duck puppet. He made a few jokes, then launched into asking questions of the small crowd gathered in the supermarket parking lot, including one which referenced something he said during his show the day before. *Yes! Here was my chance...* I flung my pudgy arm into the air, and miracle of miracles, he called on me! I knew the answer, of course, how could I not, and after shouting it out, he called me up to the stage. I trundled up the steps and stood to his right, next to Webster Webfoot, who, truth be told, was somewhat less impressive up close. At this point, Jimmy Weldon leaned toward me and said, "What's your name, son?"

Time for a brief aside. I have had people so consistently mispronounce my last name throughout my life that I have mostly given up trying to correct anyone. It even happens frequently that I will introduce myself to someone and say my name, and they will repeat it back in a mispronounced manner. What the F, I ask you? What the F, indeed. (Yes, I know WTF, it just seems funnier to write out the "What the" part). Here is where it gets interesting: I have mentioned before that my wife is an amazing elementary grade teacher, and of course she has had the same issue with the name, but she came up with an amazing workaround. She teaches the kids that "It's Buenafe, pronounced like

Beautiful." Of course, then the little children couldn't resist calling her Ms. Beautiful, and I only needed to hear her anecdote once before I began deploying the same explanation with my own students. I worked for many years as a high school administrator, and of course I was always "the cool one", as in "Just go to Buenafe and tell him what happened. He won't yell at you or anything." Well, it only took two or three "It's Buenafe, like Beautiful" incidents before the students commenced calling *me* Mr. Beautiful, which, all things considered, is not the worst thing they could have called me.

So, Jimmy Weldon leaned toward me with his evil question. I was a bit nervous and perhaps star struck, but I managed to say, "My name is Larry Buenafe."

Here's where I was gravely wounded: Jimmy Weldon, sweet, kindly man with a duck puppet, bringing joy and cartoons to thousands of kids across the central valley of California, in the loudest, most cartoonish voice ever uttered in the long, winding history of humans on earth, said, "HAIRY GOONAFAY!?!"

Well, there it is. How does a chubby, immature eight-year-old recover from that? The answer at the time was you don't, because I was too oblivious to realize he was making a joke, so I replied, "No, it's Larry Buenafe." He gave me a patronizing pat on the shoulder and continued with his routine. I don't really remember what was said after that, but here is the most perfectly pathetic part of all: Jimmy Weldon and Webster Webfoot had various sponsors, including Hormel Meats. So, for providing the correct answer to his question and mangled name chuckles at my expense, I won five pounds of bacon, which he handed me as I walked off stage. I suppose there are worse things I could have won, but I can't think of any, because from that point forward the other kids at school commenced referring to me as Hairy Goonafay, the

Bacon Boy. I took it all in feigned good humor, but I didn't really think it was all that funny, to tell the truth.

And what have we learned from this sordid tale? Never trust a man with his hand up a duck's butt.

Mother of the Year

As I mentioned before, I was a nervous, clingy, fearful child. I know, sounds like a real delight. One of the ways it manifested itself was that I had a real problem with my mother not being within eyesight; I'm sure that was no picnic for her. On one particularly embarrassing occasion, when I was eight, my dad was out somewhere, and my mom and all the kids were watching the big console TV with the vice grips attached so you could change the channel because the knob had broken. We were all sitting around in our PJs and watching our last show before bedtime, when I looked up and noticed that my mom was not there. My reaction to that might be described as somewhat irrational; it might also be described as freakin'crazy. I ran outside, into the pouring rain, and into the road; for some reason, the only possibility that came to my mind was that she must have wandered out into the night and was roaming the streets. I really was completely and utterly panicked; a car came by, and I stood in the street and flagged them down; they stopped, and rolled down the window, and I apologized for stopping them, but asked if they had seen a woman walking down the street, because my mother was gone and I didn't know where she was. They were very nice, but said no, they hadn't seen a woman walking down the street, and that I should go look for her in the house. I thanked them and apologized again, and when I turned around, saw my mother standing in the doorway; I ran and tried to explain that I didn't know where she was so I was trying to find her; I remember not understanding why she was so angry at me when I had only been trying to relieve my fear. Yuck, what an emotional mess.

I tell you that humiliating tale to set the scene for this one. Another way my body reacted to my emotions was that I regularly had a "stomach ache" in the morning when it came time to go to school, and I would frequently ask my mom if I could stay home. I wasn't lying at the time; I really did have stomach pains all those times, but they were emotional rather than gastrointestinal in origin. Nevertheless, she never allowed me to stay home unless I was demonstrably ill. So, what had happened was...

In those days, each elementary school class had a room mother; a parent volunteer who would bring cupcakes or the like on the day before a school holiday. On one such day, when I was in the fourth grade, I woke in the morning and had a terrible stomach ache, with no quotation marks this time; my stomach really hurt. Of course, I asked to stay home, and of course my mom assumed I was faking, and made me go to school. As the day progressed, my pain got worse and worse, and finally my moaning and gasping convinced my teacher that something might actually be wrong, and she sent me to the office. Upon arriving at the office, I advised the secretary of my stomach problem, and she advised me that the nurse wasn't in, but I could lie across some chairs if I wanted. Not even a bed or cot, just three molded plastic chairs to lie across, which I did.

Well, I spent all day tossing and turning on these three molded plastic chairs, but apparently, I didn't make enough noise to convince the secretary or Principal that anything much was wrong. As the day drew to a close, my mother arrived at school; she was the room mother for my brother's class. My stomach was hurting so badly that I didn't even get up to go back to my own class for the class party. When the final bell rang, I waited until I saw my mom and asked her if I could ride home with her because my stomach was hurting, but she said no and made me ride the bus home. It seems very cruel now looking back, but I suppose she had her reasons. At any rate, I got on the bus and spent the ride lying on the seat moaning; in those days, the school bus would drop you off right in front of your house, so when we arrived on Cain Street, my three siblings skipped off the bus, but I was hurting so bad that I literally fell out into the gutter. My siblings ran and told my mother that I was in the gutter, and I guess by now she assumed that there may actually be something wrong with me; she took me to the doctor, who said to get me to the hospital immediately; my appendix had burst, and my system was being flooded with toxins that were threatening to kill me if not dealt with *post haste*. I was taken in for emergency surgery and spent the next couple of days in the hospital trying to recover, while my mother spent the next couple of days trying to recover from crushing guilt (or at least I imagine she did).

There were some positive outcomes from this incident: I was a pudgy little kid before having my appendix out, but as a result I lost about 20 pounds and I just never went back; I have a really cool scar that was impressive to the other little kids; and although I didn't do it very often, if I needed to work a guilt angle with my mom I always had this situation chambered and ready to fire. Mother of the Year indeed—she tried to kill me! Alright, I don't guess she was really trying to kill me, but you never know...

The moral of this story? Although it should not be the first option, surgery can nevertheless be effective as part of a sensible weight loss plan. However, don't take things into your own hands; consult a physician first, that's the most prudent approach.

Sixth Grade Highlight Reel

I bet most people have that one teacher at some point in their schooling that really made a difference in their life. For me it was Mr. Vernon, my 6th grade teacher. Somehow, we just clicked; I changed more as a result of his class than all the rest of my schooling combined. I suppose being in the throes of puberty and multiple growth spurts added to that; whatever the case, he was a great teacher and I am better and different for having been in his class. Does anyone have a box of tissues?

I was an early bloomer physically and was taller and more athletic than most of my peers in the 6th grade. I loved playing all sports, but especially basketball and football. I had a strong arm, and in pickup football games I always played quarterback. I had the urge to be good, so I wanted to throw the football every chance I got, which meant that a lot of the time I would just throw the ball, run and pick it up, and throw it back the other way. Then I thought, if I throw it against something, say, a wall or some such contrivance, it will bounce back and there will be less time wasted running for the ball. For some reason, this then morphed into throwing it against the next-door neighbor's brick chimney. What could go wrong, right?

Here's how it would go: I would pretend that I was getting the snap from the center, then roll out to my left in the tiny front yard of our house on Cain Street, throw the ball against the neighbor's chimney, then do it again, over and over. Hundreds of times. It never occurred to me that this might be annoying to the neighbors. I honestly didn't think about it or realize that they could even hear it, or as the case was, feel it. Why would I not think about this? Because I was a stupid eleven-year-old in my own fantasy world, that's why.

One day, as I was engaged in this activity, flinging the football over and over at the neighbor's chimney, the ball slipped out of the side of my hand. There was a window next to their chimney, and the ball went through the window and into the neighbor's living room. Unfortunately, the window was closed at the time, so for the ball to make the trek into their living room, it had to break through the window, which it did. I had a moment of total panic at this point. I think if anyone had been watching, I would have looked like a mime trying to run out of an invisible cage; I ran in one direction, stopped, ran another direction, stopped, and eventually realized that there was no way to escape.

I trudged up to the neighbor's front door, met them as they were coming out, and realized at that moment that I had never met them before, and never really even seen them. I was greeted, or confronted, as the case may be, by a vaguely middle-aged lady, or at least she seemed middle aged to my 11-year-old self. She had a round, friendly face, although she wasn't happy at that moment, and she was wearing what might euphemistically be called "mom shorts" and a stretched-out tank top. I think she could see the panic in my face and probably felt a little sorry for me in that moment; her expression softened, and she asked, "What happened? This seemed like a dumb question to me, it was obvious what happened. I began babbling, "I'm terribly sorry, I was practicing, and the ball slipped out of my hand, I'll pay for the window, I'm really sorry," etc. etc. I was starting to cry a little at that point.

She got a little half smile on her face and said, "Okay, calm down. You haven't been throwing that football against our chimney, have you?"

"Well, maybe a little bit," I sniffled.

"Well no wonder stuff keeps falling off our mantle," she said. Suddenly I had a flash of painful insight: maybe I should start playing basketball instead.

Zoom forward about two months, and now we are into December. I am outside shooting baskets in the driveway in the pouring rain. Shooting baskets, over and over, for hours in the pouring rain. Hormones are a wonderful and terrible thing. Here was the problem: I was already ill when I went out to shoot baskets in the pouring rain, and over the next day or so continued to get worse. I was having trouble breathing and was coughing up huge green wads of material. Finally, my mother decided to take me to the doctor, who promptly referred me to the hospital, where an x-ray confirmed that I was suffering from what was called double pneumonia at the time. This meant that one of my lungs had collapsed and the other was half-full of material. They set me up in a hospital bed with a plastic tent over my upper body, and there I remained for a week.

The funny part of this was, aside from being painfully short of breath, I really didn't feel that bad. I probably can attribute that at least in part to the massive doses of puberty-related hormones that were flooding my body at the time. At any rate, on several occasions during my week-long stay in the hospital, when I was alone in the room, I turned over on my stomach and...did pushups, 40 at a time. You thought I was going to say something else, didn't you? Get your mind out of the gutter, you little rascal. Speaking of which, though...

Once a day, during my week-long hospital stay, one of two nurses would come in and announce that it was time to wash up. Nurse One would take a wet cloth and wipe my face and then hand me the cloth and instructed me to wipe "down there". Nurse Two, who came in twice while I was in the hospital, also wiped my face, but in addition, instead of having me wipe "down there", put her hand under the covers and wiped "down there" herself. Now, she did not linger, and this may have been more-or-less standard procedure, I wouldn't really know. All I can say is that it left me somewhat confused and yet excited in a certain way to which I was unaccustomed. I think she knew it too, although I have nothing with which to verify this. Nevertheless, she was, and remains, my all-time favorite nurse.

What is the moral of this story? When considering careers that might be best for you, you could do worse than a career in the area of health care. Helping people in so many different ways is highly rewarding.

Let Us In!

My biological family has always been relatively clean-living. Both of my parents smoked like chimneys on a cold winter's night, but neither were drinkers, and there was never any alcohol in the house. There were other problems, poor eating habits being especially notable, but I have four siblings and none of us ever really got around to getting into drugs or alcohol.

For a number of years, when we were young, my parents belonged to a Pinochle club with about ten other couples, and once a month they would go to the house of one of the couples for a Pinochle club party. Often, they would be theme parties, and I remember one party held at our house in which all the couples came dressed as "hoboes", complete with torn clothes, handkerchiefs on sticks, etc. The only time I ever saw my parents drink alcohol was at these parties; my dad would always order a Harvey Wallbanger, probably only because he thought the name was funny.

You get the picture that we as a family, and especially the children, didn't really have any experience with alcohol. However, when I was in the seventh grade we moved to "the good side of town", and I soon had a new group of friends who could be described as somewhat more 'worldly' than me. I quickly became best friends with Lonnie Crusher, who lived just a few houses down from our new house on the good side of town, and whose parents did decidedly have a taste for alcohol. There were bottles secreted away all over the place, and I spent a lot of time at their house. I didn't partake of any of the alcohol, but I was around it quite a lot, and on one occasion Lonnie pulled a bottle of Vermouth out of an end table in the family room that his father had hidden. Lonnie's father was one of the most jovial people I have ever met; he always called me Larry from Tucumcari, and would pretend to want to box with me constantly. Maybe part of his loquaciousness had to do with the fact that he was part snockered most of the time, I don't know. At any rate, we snuck around to a part of the house where we would be undetected, and both took a sip (well, I took a sip—Lonnie took a hearty pull). My thought: "Yuck! Why would anyone drink this crap?" I was so naïve, I didn't know at the time that people drank alcohol for reasons other than the taste, but I was to learn soon enough...

Another of my best friends in those days was a kid named Jackie Kravitz. He came from what I would describe as a chaotic family situation. He had a passel of siblings, all living in a rather dilapidated home in a relatively nice area. His parents were divorced, and his father was a successful person, so he would show up every so often, each time in a different sports car, while Jackie and the rest of the family tooled around in an old VW bus. There was practically no furniture in the house, and all the beds sat on the floor. They did have a piano and a record player, though, and we spent lots of time listening and pretending to play. There was always a ruckus going on in the Kravitz house; these folks were very bright, but wild, which is often a bad combination. Jackie's mom was... interesting, I guess you might say. She caused quite an uproar in town by writing an article that was published in Playgirl magazine, which featured **gasp**naked men instead of women. My mom had a copy of the issue, which she kept "hidden" in a drawer by the phone, which, as hiding places go, was pretty crappy. This makes me a bit queasy to say it, but I think my mom may have had a bit of a horny streak. *Gross.*

On one occasion, I was at the Kravitz house sitting at the piano, trying to work my way through Moonlight Sonata, and Ms. Kravitz came over to sit next to me. She listened for a minute or two, and said, "You are so talented. Did you know that?" She smiled at me and put her hand on my shoulder, which made me deeply uncomfortable, but not enough that I would ask her to remove it—I would have been even more uncomfortable doing something that could be perceived as rude. I don't know if she felt my discomfort or not, but she smiled and said, "Oh, you don't need to worry about any Mrs. Robinson situation with me, I just enjoy listening."

Why did she have to say that? Up to that point it would never have entered my mind, but now she put it in there and it can't be undone! AAAH! I fidgeted in unbearable discomfort, and after a moment, said "Well, thanks Ms. Kravitz. I guess it's time to head home," and bolted for the door.

"Oh, stop with the Ms. Kravitz stuff," she laughed, "You know you can just call me Margie."

I stopped at the door, turned, and said "Okay, Ms. Kravitz, will do," and ran for home with the speed of Mercury, with little wings on my feet.

Across the street from the Kravitz' lived Grubby Sharp. He was a year younger than Jackie and me, but he was precocious, and an equal in terms of wildness to the Kravitz clan. Grubby had a brother who was quite a bit older who knew how to play guitar, so we would occasionally go to the Sharp house to listen to him jam. Directly next door to the Sharps lived a man who drove a beer delivery truck. Think you know what happens next? Yeah, that happened, but there's more to the story...

Grubby somehow stole a keg of beer out of his neighbor's truck and invited all the neighborhood boys to come over on a Friday night. We knew that we needed to take it somewhere if it was to be consumed without being caught, so Grubby put it in a trash can and it was hauled to a nearby nine-hole pitch and putt golf course and dragged onto the seventh green. There we sat, a group of seven or eight freshmen in high school, with a stolen keg on private property. I didn't drink any of the beer aside from a quick taste; I didn't like it at all, and couldn't imagine how anyone else could, but the other boys more than made up for my restraint. Lonnie and Jackie were among the group, and both were consuming copious amounts. It was late fall, and heavy fog had settled on the area, making it impossible for anyone to see us, although they very likely could hear us, especially as more of the beer got consumed.

Suddenly, Jackie said "Hey, a bunch of girls are having a slumber party over at Julie Jackson's house. They're in the garage; let's go over there and try to get them to let us in!" Like all hair-brained schemes, this sounded pretty good to us, so we left the keg on the green and trotted the half mile or so over to Julie's house. She lived on a small farm, with a couple of horses in front in a pen that led back forty yards or so to the house and the object of our desire, the garage. The thick fog made a perfect cover, and we hid behind a small barn about fifteen yards away from the garage trying to work up the courage to go and make contact. Finally, Jackie said, "Well, I don't know about you chickens, but I'm going," and stood up and headed for the garage. I followed close behind, but the rest of the group stayed by the barn, apparently unwilling or unable to stumble drunkenly toward the garage. Jackie and I crept up to the garage, and he began tapping on the garage door, whispering, "Hey! It's me, Jackie. Let us in!"

From inside the garage, I could hear the girls giggling, and Julie said "No! Go away!'

Well, Jackie was having none of it; he began tapping harder and being more insistent, saying, in a louder voice, "Let us in! Let's make out!" The girls were equally insistent that we leave *with great haste.* Finally, Jackie stood up and began pounding on the aluminum garage door, making a booming sound, and yelling "LET US IN! WE WANT SOME SNATCH!" For those of you not familiar with that term, it is a synonym for "*pussy*", an expletive a recent president is apparently fond of, which is of course a synonym for "*vagina*". Note that we were freshmen in high school; none of us had any previous experience with "*snatch*", but as you may know, lack of experience has never stopped boys from talking about it, and certainly never stopped Jackie from yelling about it, especially in his somewhat inebriated state.

The girls continued to try to shoo us away, but finally Jackie reached down and began pulling up the garage door, and as it rose to its up position, it revealed Julie's dad standing there, pointing a shotgun at us. I probably don't need to tell you this was decidedly a buzz kill. Jackie and I looked at each other, and, calculating that Julie's dad was not likely to actually shoot us, turned and sprinted for all we were worth, and quickly disappeared in the dense fog. We ran through the streets, all the way back to the golf course, but never saw the other guys. Then, a crucial mistake: I let Jackie talk me into going back to Julie's house to rescue the others, who we assumed had been captured by Julie's dad. How we were going to rescue them was unclear; we didn't think that far ahead, we just began jogging back toward the house. We turned a corner near their horse barn, and came face to face with Shotgun Dad, who said, "Okay, boys, walk this way." *Oh no, we are going to the firing squad.* Jackie turned to say something, which momentarily distracted Shotgun Dad, and I saw that as my moment to escape; I turned and sprinted off, this time heading for home. Shotgun Dad yelled, "*Hey, come back here you little shit!*" But I was gone, daddy, long gone.

The fog was so thick that it was not easy to make out faces, even of those very near, and I was banking on the fact that Shotgun Dad didn't know me, or at least didn't see me well enough to know who I was, which turned out to be true. Aside from mortal fear, here is where I was hurt on this excursion: it was so foggy I ran headlong into a barbed wire fence at a full sprint and was sent sprawling backward. Although I was hurting bad, I didn't have time to take stock, I just had to keep moving at that point. On my way home I ran into Lonnie, who had also eluded capture, and we went, him stumbling and me limping, down our street.

When we arrived at my house, we stopped for a moment to check my injuries. I had ripped the thigh area of both my pant legs, and my shirt in the chest area, and I had significant gashes at all three of those locations from my contact with the barbed wire fence and was covered with blood. “Holy crap, look at you!” Lonnie slurred; I looked over to see him lying in the gutter, pointing and snickering. Then he looked up in the night sky, and said, “Look at the stars! They’re going around in circles!” I helped him up from the gutter and guided him to his house, while he continued to snicker, saying “Man, you got jacked up!” So much for best friends.

I got him home and dropped him in his front yard, turned and limp/jogged for home. Somehow, I was able to hide my wounds from my parents, and the other guys didn’t rat me out, so I was able to avoid the severe penalties I would have had to pay if my parents had discovered the full extent of our activities on that fateful night.

So, let’s recount: theft; trespassing, twice; underage consumption of alcohol; possible sexual harassment; drunk in public; I think that about covers it. Not bad for a night’s work. Of course, most of those were not committed by me directly, but I was certainly along for the ride.

So, what is the moral of this story? Well, AA might be a good place to start.

Basketballhead/Mother of the Year, Part Two

We know that human brains don't stop developing until approximately the early 20's; based on behavior, some would argue it's much later than that. We also know that the portion of the brain that takes the longest to fully develop is the area called the prefrontal cortex, which is largely responsible for control of impulses and decision-making. This at least in part explains why otherwise intelligent teenagers, do stunningly stupid, impulsive things; however, it doesn't come close to explaining the following.

Summer is, for most Americans, a great time of the year. School is out, the weather is warm (or really hot here in the central valley of California), nights are awesome, and hanging out with friends is even better. When you are 15, having a friend who is 16 is a must, so that you can drive around and experience the first blushes of freedom before being crushed, a few short years later, by the responsibilities of adulthood.

For many, including me, it was simultaneously the best and worst time in life; like many teenagers, I was hyper-aware of every flaw, perceived or real, and imagined that EVERYONE could see the big zit between my eyes and was judging me unworthy. Of course, I didn't quite have the insight at that age to realize that most people my age were similarly self-obsessed, and only had a passing interest in anything so trivial as another person. It's interesting how this self-obsession manifests; I suppose it has to do with how things are in the biological family, as you get the whole spectrum from kids who have irrationally high self-esteem (think the kid who somehow becomes student body president, while possessing at 2.0 GPA) to anorexics and cutters, and everything in between. I think my outward appearance at that time would have been on the higher end of that scale, but my inward experience was that I was trying to prove that I wasn't the piece of crap that I knew I was by being an achiever. I know, really funny. What does all that have to do with Basketballhead? Calm down, I'm getting to it...

It was a very warm Friday evening, about nine pm, and it was time to socialize. Somehow three friends and I ended up at the east end of Green Gables Drive; this was where the rich people lived in our town. We were parked on the street and chatting about stealing some toilet paper from the Green Gables Country Club, just a couple of blocks away, so that we could toilet paper the house of a friend that lived just a few houses down from where we were at the time; you know, good, wholesome activity for a Friday night. My best friend at the time, Burt Dillwad (you may be surprised to know that is not his real name) and I were sitting on the trunk of the car, while the designated sixteen-year-old friend was in the driver's seat talking to the fourth of our group of future Nobel Prize winners. There we were, chatting amiably, planning our activities, when Designated Sixteen-Year-Old decided that it would be really funny to start driving with Burt and me sitting on the trunk, and it goes without saying that Burt and I thought it would be really funny if we held on and went for a ride. In retrospect, this was a choice that I would now describe as less than ideal. We careened around the corner and onto Green Gables Drive going about 20 MPH; Burt jumped off at that point, deciding that getting a little skinned up was better than getting a little killed; I hung on, assuming Designated Sixteen-Year-Old would stop sometime soon.

He stopped alright, right after I slipped and fell from the trunk at twenty-five MPH. That may not sound that fast, but you try falling face-first onto the pavement from a car trunk at that speed and see how well you do. Here is where the name that followed me in certain circles of friends, and persisted throughout my high school years, came from; When I contacted the road with my face, I *bounced several feet into the air several times* before coming to rest face down on the street. An important note: Green Gables Drive, and the surrounding area, was an island in the middle of town, in that it was technically not in the city limits; obviously, this was because all the rich people did not want to pay city taxes, etc., and were influential enough to keep their area out of the city. One of the results of this was that they did not have some of the city services, such as streetlights, so where I fell and came to rest was very dark, it being nighttime and all. I remember slipping and falling, seeing the ground rush up to meet my face, a very brief moment of pain, and then...nothing, at least for a while.

Burt came running up, fearing trouble from the residents of the area, and, not realizing the extent of my injuries, kicked me in the side, saying "Come on, get up! We gotta get outta here!" Of course, I didn't hear that, it was described to me later; at the moment I was hearing nothing. When I didn't get up, he rolled me over, and, seeing that all the skin was gone from my face, went into a panicked dance. At that point I started convulsing, amplifying the panic; he was already a jumpy, hyperactive kid, and I just imagine he would have been comical to watch in that moment if I could have done so. They quickly ran to a nearby house, this being far removed from the days of cell phones in every pocket, and an ambulance soon arrived. I awoke as I was being put on a stretcher, and tried to say, "I'm okay, I can get up", but that's not exactly what came out; it was more like IIIIIMMEICICHFIHINELEMNIJND<M." I remember hearing myself trying to say the words, and thinking, "Hey, that's not what I said," and then I was out again.

The next time I was conscious, I noticed, as I opened my eyes, that I was in a very bright room with people and machines and beeping noises in the background. The people seemed to be huddled around me, and were wearing odd clothing; I remember hearing an occasional *plink!*, which sounded to me like a little pebble being dropped into a metal container. Then I realized that what I was hearing was *little pebbles being dropped into a metal container*, and the little pebbles were *coming from my face*. That was decidedly not cool. Then I was out again...

I woke up sometime the next day, which was now Saturday, not feeling all that well. I didn't have any broken bones, but I also didn't have much undamaged skin left on my face; additionally, I had a very large cut on the back of my head and a very major concussion. In fact, it took quite a while for me to remember what even happened. My family members were in the hospital room, although seemingly not very happy about it, and my friends were rather conspicuously absent. It may have been that they were not welcome, but it's more likely that they wanted to stay as far away as possible so as to avoid any further repercussions.

As mentioned, this was a Saturday; despite my injuries and concussion, I was allowed to go home the following day, now Sunday. Earlier I mentioned that this occurred during the summer; what I didn't mention was that I was enrolled in summer school at the time, taking World History. On Monday, despite my face being one large scab, despite having the back of my head shaved and stitches appearing there; despite having just had a very major concussion, my mother made me go to summer school. You may be getting the idea from these stories that I had a conflicted relationship with my mother, and partly that's true, but she was right; if you are going to be stupid, then you must take the consequences of being stupid, which I unhappily did. I can laugh at myself, and I did, and embraced the name Basketballhead proudly.

My joke, as I tell people this story, is that before this incident, I had an IQ of 180, but because of my brain injury my IQ went all the way down to 160. But that's not true—it's still 180. (Okay, that's not true either, but it's a decent joke).

The moral of this story? Stay away from Green Gables Drive. It's a scary, scary place. It's haunted, so the legend goes; haunted by the *ghost of Basketballhead...*

My Foot, and Other Things That Blow Up

Why do boys like to blow things up? Oh, sure, I know there are some girls who like this as well, but to physically break things and literally cause things to explode is, I think you'll agree, primarily a male activity. I did a little research on the subject, and one theory seemed intuitively correct to me: that blowing things up is what is described as "potlatch" behavior. In other words, it is mainly the domain of those who do not experience want or need; therefore, the act of destroying things is enjoyable because it is done without fear of deprivation. People who want for some of the more basic needs in life are not as likely to enjoy such demolition because they perceive it as wasteful, and it represents a lost opportunity to relieve some of their need.

I know that was true for me; I never understood it when other kids would throw food, or break something intentionally, and I had no experience with anything incendiary beyond maybe a fourth of July sparkler. I didn't even like lighting a match, to be honest. Where is this going, you ask? Did you read the title?

I had the good fortune of being relatively good at sports in high school, which in part meant that my group of friends sometimes included other athletic types, including Robbie Ortega, who went on to pitch in the major leagues for a number of years. He was certainly good in high school, but kind of a doofus, and I would not have guessed that he would make it that far, to be honest. He lived on the opposite side of town, in what I would have described as the rich side, although to me anything middle class or up seemed extravagant. So, one sunny spring Saturday several of my friends and I were cruising around, which people did in those days; I was in the front passenger seat with two friends in the back and Tim Carey, a particularly sketchy member of our little social circle, driving. Someone in the car, one of the guys in the back, I think, produced an M-80, which is a much larger and more powerful version of a firecracker. Urban legend has it that an M-80 is equivalent to a quarter of a stick of dynamite, but it's not true. I even looked it up, which qualifies as twice that I have researched for this story. I'll wait for you to finish being impressed. Now, I had never seen an M-80 before, and didn't really have a good sense of what it could do, but when you're cruising around with your bros and you're sixteen years old, your daring just gets cranked up to levels to which it would not normally go.

Tim, being the devious sort that he was, said, "Let's go by Robbie's house and throw it out in his front yard. His old man will have a shit fit!", which was a phrase that people used back then; seems almost quaint now, doesn't it? So, off we scuttled toward the good side of town, M-80 at the ready. As we pulled to a stop in front of the house, one of the brainiacs in the back seat discovered that, in this particular piece of vehicular crap, the rear windows did not roll down. My window was down, and the curb was on the passenger side, so the Einstein in the rear passenger side attempted to throw the M-80, with its now lit fuse, out my window, which would have resulted in hilarity and screeching tires, except that it thudded off the chrome strip at the top of the door and bounced back into the car, landing on the floorboard at my feet.

I don't suppose I need to tell you that this was problematic. Now, normally I am good in stressful moments, but this was an exception to that rule. I tried stomping on it, thinking... not thinking at all, actually, just panicking; it exploded, instantly filling the car with smoke and probably permanently damaging all of our ears; we threw the doors open and fell out into the street, coughing and choking; I realized that I was feeling pain in my foot, and glanced down to see the end of my shoe and sock were gone, and one of my toes was red with blood. Robbie and his father were out of their house by then, and when they finally stopped laughing his father got a hose and squirted my foot. The high-pitched whistling in my ears blocked out whatever they were saying, which was probably for the best, because I don't think it was particularly flattering. I suppose in a way I was lucky; it could easily have blown my toe off, but instead just left it somewhat mangled. Somehow, I was able to hide this injury from my parents, although I don't think they would have been particularly concerned if they had known, to tell the truth. I can just hear my dad: "Way to go, dummy." And my mom: "Don't get any blood on the carpet."

And the moral of this story? Pick better friends, obviously. Maybe the choir kids; they almost never try to make you explode. Oh, and sturdy footwear.

I Hate Sadie Hawkins

Pain comes in various forms, not all of which are physical. Although physical pain is usually more acute, emotional pain can potentially be more lasting. Among the powerful forms of emotional pain are humiliation and embarrassment, both of which are featured prominently in the following.

In general, teenage boys are socially inept when it comes to managing themselves around teenage girls. They do tend to learn quickly what girls will and will not accept, and tend to stay within those boundaries, based on their powerful desire to be close to said girls. I'm not completely sure how or why, but the message that I got was to protect my emotional self vigorously and avoid any risk of rejection. At the same time, I was very fond of girls, and desirous of closeness with girls, which put me in a bit of a conundrum. I would never approach a girl in any more than a casually friendly way, despite any interest I might have in the girl, unless I had a very good idea that the girl was interested in me first. For example, if my best friend Burt Dillwad came to me and said, "Hey, man, that girl likes you", or if a girl came up to me and said, "Hey, man, I like you", or if a girl hired a skywriter to write, "Hey, man, I like you", and then pointed to me as it was being written across the sky, and then winked and offered me a piece of candy, then I might work up the nerve to talk to her.

I got better as time went on, but in my teenage years that's how it was. I might have been good at hiding it, but that was my internal experience. To compound matters, I was terrible at talking to girls. I just didn't know what to say, and I was deathly afraid of saying something embarrassing, so I would just avoid such situations. So, imagine my surprise when, in my sophomore year, I was approached by a girl who very much wanted me to be her boyfriend. I had no ability to say no to this, nor did I want to; she was a very nice girl from a nice family, and we embarked on a four-year long relationship, lasting until the end of my freshman year in college and the end of her senior year in high school. The time frame is important because...

Toward the end of my senior year, I got to know a girl from the other high school in town, let's call her Diane, because she was taking a class at our school and we sat next to one another in the class. She was very nice, and very cute, and we would chat a little bit in class. What I didn't know was that she had developed a bit of a crush on me, but I found out when, one day after class, she asked me to go to the Sadie Hawkins dance with her. As you probably know, many schools and districts have an annual Sadie Hawkins dance, with the central conceit being that the girls ask the boys instead of the other way around. Did you know that this originated from a comic strip all the way back in the 1930's, in which a father, in hopes of marrying off his homely daughter, set up a contest in which the eligible bachelors in town would have a foot race, with his daughter running after them, and if she caught one of them, that one would have to marry the homely daughter? And of course, her name was Sadie Hawkins, and somehow the original story was forgotten and morphed into what we have today. Well, after that brief history lesson...

Honestly, I was caught off-guard and didn't know what to say. What I should have said was "Oh, that would really be nice, and thank you, but I have a girlfriend, and it wouldn't be right for me to go with someone else to the Sadie Hawkins dance." What I did say was "Sure." My next thought: "Oh crap." Why did I say yes? And now what do I do? Oh, *crap crap crap*. Hang on, friends, this is not even close to the worst part.

For the next week my stomach was completely in knots, and I suppose that I was engaging in some magical thinking, figuring that if I ignore that very large monster in the closet it will just go away, but it didn't. In fact, it just got *bigger and more monster-y*. A few days before the dance, my girlfriend confronted me about being asked to the dance, and I came clean, and told her that I just said yes because I didn't know what to say, which was partly true, and that I was not going to go. She was more-or-less understanding, being the nice girl from a nice family that she was, but of course I had now put myself in a completely untenable situation.

On the day before the dance, I spoke to Diane on the phone. She was very excited, talking about her plans for the evening. I took a deep breath—okay, here goes... "Well, see, Diane, something has come up, and my parents are going out of town to the coast, and I have to go with them. I'm really sorry." Well, there it is, I am officially a whale turd. To make matters worse, Diane was her sweet self, being all understanding, saying it was okay, we would maybe get together another time, etc. Oh, crap. *Crap crap crap*. I just verified that my self-loathing is well-deserved.

We said our goodbyes, and fast forward to the next night, the night of the dance. My girlfriend was out of town (the reason I was available to go to the Sadie Hawkins dance in the first place), and to escape my disgust with myself, I went for a ride with a group of friends. In those days, people still did some cruising on a Friday night, and we were doing just that when we pulled up to the busiest intersection in town. We were at the stoplight, going straight, and were next to the left turn lane. I was in the rear driver-side seat, nearest the cars in the left turn lane. As we were waiting for the light to change, I glanced to my left at the car next to us, and there was Diane, looking at me through the car window. She didn't even look angry; bemused would be a better description. What did I do? What any good whale turd would do, I *ducked down*, hoping she didn't see me. I just prayed for the light to change, and after about seven years, or thirty seconds, I'm not sure which, it did, and we drove on.

Somehow, nothing seemed to come of this situation. No one talked about it, and things just went on as if it never happened. Obviously, I never got over it, or I wouldn't be writing about it here, under the heading of Emotional Pain, Humiliation and Embarrassment subtype. And then, the final insult: I ran into Diane three years later. I was turning a corner, walking across my college campus, and practically ran into her. I didn't know she was a student there, but there is no particular reason I would have known, it being a big school on a big campus. At any rate, of course she was sweet and friendly, asking how I was and what I had been up to with a huge, sincere smile on her face. She was genuinely happy to see me, and of course never mentioned the dance, seeing me on that night, etc. It would have been so much easier if she had cussed me out and called me names, but no, she had to twist the knife by being sweet. And, she was not trying to kill me with kindness, which I at least could have appreciated for the punishment it would have inflicted, she was simply being herself. On second thought, I suppose the obvious juxtaposition between angel and whale turd was punishment enough.

What is the moral of this story? In the immortal words of Socrates, the unexamined life is not worth living. And also, Sadie Hawkins is a bitch.

High Rolling

There was a brief moment in history when the roller-skating rink was the coolest place in the universe. There was also a moment when Disco was king of the music world; not surprisingly, those two trends shared the same moment. I hated Disco at the time, and I had no idea how to skate, coming from a family that didn't have the money for such extravagances as roller skates. Nevertheless, there I was, right in the middle of it all; I had a friend who worked at Roller City, the mecca for local skating and Disco, and he let me know that he was quitting. Despite my lack of skating skills and distaste for Disco, I decided to apply, as it definitely sounded better than my job at the time—Pallet Repairman for Williams Business Forms. Yes, that deserves some explanation.

I had another friend who worked for Williams Business Forms; the name of the company was not euphemistic at all—they made forms for businesses. The plant consisted of a huge warehouse in an industrial park with thick concrete walls, lots of large and noisy machines, gigantic rolls of paper, and pallets. Lots and lots of pallets. So many pallets that it seemed as if they were intent on causing a world-wide shortage by hoarding them all, thus driving up the pallet price. I didn't know any of this when my friend encouraged me to apply for the position of Pallet Repairman; in fact, I didn't really know what a pallet was. Nevertheless, I needed a job, and for some reason they hired me. If any of you have worked in a factory environment before, you know it is a bit of a world unto itself; aside from office staff, the workers were 100% male, and when that happens things can get...weird. I suppose places with 100% female employees can get weird too, but I bet it's not the same kind of weird. In places with 100% male employees, there's a lot of spitting, farting, and perhaps surprisingly, a lot of mock homoerotic talk. There were frequent calls of "Blow me!", and responses of "If I did it would be the best you ever had!" and the like. It all made me uncomfortable, and I didn't really participate, although I did occasionally laugh; if that makes me a bad person then I guess I'm a bad person.

At any rate, my job as Pallet Repairman went like this: I was in a huge room, perhaps forty feet square, with a fifteen-foot ceiling, a huge sliding metal door to allow forklifts to bring stacks of broken pallets into the room, and a workbench with an industrial, air-powered nail gun. My job was to take pallets off the stacks one by one, remove the broken boards, put new boards in their place, and nail them on using the nail gun. As you can imagine, this eventually became utterly mind-numbing; I was essentially alone for the length of my shift, aside from other workers occasionally speeding by my sliding door on forklifts. Eventually the forklift fellows knew to duck as they drove by, as I took to shooting at them with my nail gun. It really wouldn't shoot very far, only fifteen feet or so, and they weren't in any danger of being hit by flying nails, but it was still fun and served to break up at least a little of the monotony for me and for them. On one occasion, I "accidentally" shot myself in the leg with the nail gun; to this day I am not sure I even felt it when it happened, I was that numb and dead inside from my work.

Well, after a year of that, I was ready for something, anything, else, so I jumped at the opportunity for a career as Skate Guard/DJ. For some unknown reason they decided to hire me, and I quickly developed high-level skating skills. Some things I didn't know about roller skating rinks before going to work at one:

1. They rent out their rinks on certain nights of the week to different churches. Pentecostal Night was a particular favorite; women with huge beehive hairdos and long skirts skating around the rink was quite a sight. They had a particular fondness for southern gospel vocal group music, and we only had about four such records, so there was a constant stream of beehives requesting the Crabb Family, and I remember thinking that seemed like interspecies mingling.

2. There are people who do figure skating on roller skates. I am not kidding. They have (or at least they had) competitions and everything. They wore the outfits just like ice skaters—guys in weird stretchy tuxes and girls in the little short skirt outfits, and they put these stretchy fabric covers over their skates when they performed. Really. If you did this, I'm not trying to make fun of you, but you have to admit, it's kind of funny.

3. Girls who go to skating rinks like guys who work at skating rinks, as long as they are fairly normal-looking. I know, I was surprised too. It's not exactly an illustrious position, so go figure.

Now to the story. I had a group of friends and coworkers who might have been described as somewhat less than savory, who frequented the skating rink. And by frequented, I mean every day. Some of these comprise the infamous "Melvyns Gang"; I'll talk about them in a later story. How did I get mixed up with these unsavory types? Bad judgment and low self-esteem—does it every time.

Every once in a while, after getting done at about one a.m. on a Saturday night, this group of heathens and I would drive from the rink to a spot in Sequoia National Park called Hospital Rock, so named because the indigenous Native Americans considered it a place with special healing powers, so naturally, we put a road and camping area right on top of it. All right, I know I'm editorializing. At any rate, it was about a two-hour drive from the rink to Hospital Rock, and about midway in the trip we would pass Kaweah Lake, a man-made lake filled, appropriately enough, by the Kaweah River. The road to Hospital Rock follows Kaweah River all the way up to and beyond Hospital Rock, and the road is windy and steep—on one side of the road it plunges down to the river, and on the other side it continues up at a similarly steep angle. Why would we drive to Hospital Rock at three in the morning, you ask? Well, here's where it gets bizarrely stupid; a few of the more daring of the unsavories would skate from Hospital Rock to Kaweah Lake, plunging down the steep and windy road at up to thirty-five MPH. Yes, of course, I was one of them.

On the night in question, two other unsavories and I had decided to make the trek; there were a couple of issues that need to be explained to set the stage. One: when you are going downhill at thirty-five MPH, you can't stop until the road levels out somewhat—you can't even stand up at that speed. The required technique involved squatting down to lower the center of gravity and to make the fall shorter if you were so unlucky. Two: because it was the middle of the night, and obviously there are no lights on this mountain road, we needed the lights of a vehicle, following closely behind, to allow us to see where we were going. This is a vital detail.

The downhill trip started off well enough; we were cruising along, squatting down during the steep parts, when we hit a particularly steep portion of the road. I was slightly ahead of the other two, so I didn't see when one of the two fell, nor did I see the other fellow fall on purpose to check to see if the first faller was okay. What I did see, when I turned the corner, was pitch black; naturally, the vehicle had to stop to keep from running over the tumbled two, leaving me quite literally in the dark. In the space of a quarter of a second, I realized the following:

1. I was either going to plunge to my death down a literal cliff, or smash into the side of a mountain if I continued, as I could not see which way the road turned.

2. I was totally and completely boned.

I really couldn't see any other options, so what I did was sit down. I skidded on my behind for about twenty-five yards before smacking into the guard rail on the side of the cliff, bouncing off of it and landing on my back in the middle of the road. My first thought: "Oh, I'm not dead." My second thought: "Oh, *my ass is on fire!*" I could feel that something very wrong had happened back there; I stood up on wobbly legs, and saw that my sweat pants (yes, I was wearing sweat pants, I already told you I was stupid) had disappeared from the top of my behind to the backs of my knees, and that a significant portion of asphalt now resided where my skin had previously been. About that time, the truck came around the corner, and after the other unsavories stopped laughing at me I got in the back of the truck and did the best I could to hold the remnants of my sweatpants together for the ride home. As a result of this excursion I had black streaks on the backs of my legs that, although now faded, persisted for many years. By the way, I was wearing the clunky, buff-colored leather rink skates with the clay wheels that I took from the skating rink for this trip, naturally.

The moral of the story? Proper equipment is very important for any athletic endeavor, wheels attached or no. Get on it, people; spend the money, you won't regret it.

Lower Me Down

You have heard me mention the Melvyns Gang before. I am still not ready to tell you their story yet, and I'm not sure I even want to, because for me it is the worst of all these sordid tales. As you may remember, the members of that notorious group and I had a brief period of association via the also aforementioned Roller City. I found them amusing in a reckless, on-the-verge-of-out-of-control sort of way. You may have had some friends like that—exciting to be around, partially because of the specter of danger always lurking nearby. Again, low self-esteem and bad judgment lead to negative consequences, and this story is good evidence of that.

I also mentioned an area in the National Park not too far from our town called Hospital Rock. The Kaweah River runs below and past Hospital Rock, and there is a short but steep hike down to the river. I enjoyed hiking down and walking along the river heading downstream for a mile or two and making the much longer and more strenuous climb up from the river. Sounds pretty cool so far, right? Not so cool when you have the Melvyns Gang with you...

We made our way to Hospital Rock on a Saturday afternoon and were planning on the hike I just described. On the way down to the river is a path that winds around a huge boulder about thirty feet tall, and if one were to rappel down from the top of this boulder, one would land on a delightful sandy beach on the shore of the river. Of course, you could take the path down to the same spot, but where is the fun in that?

As we were standing on top of the boulder, I mentioned my thought about rappelling down to the beach instead of taking the path around, and one of the Melvynites (okay, that could be a soul group from the sixties) produced a length of rope from his backpack. Well, at that point how could I be dissuaded? You're right, I could not. As you could probably guess, I had no prior experience with such matters, but I had seen many examples of such things from watching TV, and it didn't seem that difficult...

If you were really stupid and thought about how to lower yourself down using a rope, you might think of tying the rope around your chest, or maybe tying a knot in the rope and just hanging onto the knot while you are lowered down. It takes a special kind of stupid to take the rope and run it through all the belt loops of your jean shorts, which is of course what I did. With five Melvynites at the other end of the rope, I scooted off the edge of the rock and was immediately greeted by my shorts up around my armpits and a severe pain in my nether region (or as my wife might call it, my "crotchal area"). I screamed, "*Aahhh! Go! Let me down!*" At this the Melvynites began laughing, and my descent rapidly picked up speed; another way to put it is that they dropped the rope, and me along with it. I plummeted the remaining 20 feet or so, slamming into the thankfully sandy area below.

I had the wind knocked out of me, but otherwise was not injured as a result of my fall. However, I was feeling a significant pain in my "crotchal area" (or "ballular zone", if you prefer), but even more in the location just below that most tender of districts. In that area is a crease of flesh I have heard called the "taint": a little fold between the gonadular province and anus. Sorry for all the indelicate descriptions and for using all this technical jargon, but the need to be descriptive outweighs the need for discretion in this case. At any rate, upon inspection it was clear that some ripping had occurred, which was extremely disconcerting. The seam of the jean shorts had impacted the taint with such force that a split about two inches long had opened up, and blood was dripping out. Blood Dripping Taint—great name for a Scandinavian death metal band.

After guffawing heartily, the Melvynites scampered down the trail, realizing that dropping me twenty feet instead of lowering me down may have resulted in harm, and found me doubled over like a squirrel guarding his nuts (by now you may be suspecting that I only told this story to see how many synonyms to testicles I could get into a story, which may or may not be true). At any rate, of course we had nothing with which to bandage the affected area, except for a beach towel with a picture of Elvis on it, so I had no choice but to wrap my stone garden, diaper-style, with the hunka hunka burnin love (look, you know by now there is no way I could resist that). And yes, we completed the hike as planned.

The moral of this story? Look, testicles are just funny, no matter how you slice them.

It's a Geyser!

From as early as I can remember, I always loved music. It just spoke to me down deep, at some level beyond verbal expression. I remember being a really young child, sitting in church, listening to the pipe organ, hearing all the overtones, feeling it vibrate in my body. As a youngster, I would sing along in a high, clear tone, and as I got older, I continued to sing in that high, clear tone, because I thought that was how you were supposed to do it. When Mr. Clifford, the middle school choir teacher, came to our school to recruit students from the sixth-grade classes for choir for the following year, I went in and auditioned, along with a number of other students. When he came to me and asked me to sing the notes he was playing on the piano, I did it perfectly, except that I did it in a high, lilting falsetto instead of full voice, because I thought that was how you were supposed to sing. It's not that my voice hadn't changed; I was a little bit ahead of many of my peers in that regard. Mr. Clifford grinned patiently and showed me how he wanted me to sing for him, and I was easily able to do it, so I did.

I was good at singing; I won awards and everything. But what I really wanted, especially as I got into 8th grade and beyond, was to be in an honest-to-God, real rock and roll band. I wanted that more than just about anything. My good friend, Burt Dillwad, had an older brother who played bass in a popular local band, and they came and played at our 8th grade dance (I guess they couldn't have been that successful if they were playing at the 8th grade dance). In those days, there is no way that you would have a DJ at a school dance; that would have been considered completely lame. Burt and I stood next to the stage, jamming to the music, and the piano player was so tickled by this that she handed us some percussion instruments and then we really started jamming. Good times!

When I was a senior in high school, I had my first experience at being part of a real band. I had some friends who were a year or two older and had a band. Once in a while I would go and listen to them rehearse, and I could see that they struggled with some of the singing. Of course, I volunteered to help out, and pretty soon I was singing the high parts of some of the songs; I still knew how to sing with the high voice I used as a kid, but I had learned the additional trick of adding some grit so that it had a rock sound. In those days every band had to play Stairway to Heaven, and the guitar player in the band wanted to sing it badly but he couldn't do the high part at the end, so he would sing the beginning of the song, and I would come in when the screaming started. I did exactly one gig with this group, a backyard party, as I remember, and then lost track of them. As it turns out, that was probably for the best.

As I have mentioned before, we weren't a family that had a lot of money for extra things, and I knew if I wanted to be in a band long term, I would have to learn how to play an instrument of some kind. I was never able to pull that together until a year after graduating from high school, when I was working at the previously mentioned mecca for skating and Disco, Roller City. I got to know a group of guys from a nearby town who would come into the rink fairly regularly; they told me they had a band but were having trouble finding a bass player. My response to that?

"Hey, I play bass!" I didn't play bass; I could play a few chords on guitar, but I had no idea about bass, and didn't even know how to tune one. What I did know was that I really wanted to be in a band, and here was my opportunity. We set up an audition for the following week, and they gave me a few songs to learn, so I had one week to: 1. Get a bass guitar. 2. Get an amp through which to play the bass guitar. 3. Learn how to play bass guitar. Nothing to it, right?

I had a friend who had a bass and amp, so I went the next day to see him, and somehow, I talked him into lending me his bass and amp. Problems 1 and 2 solved, at least short-term. As I mentioned, I didn't know how to tune a bass, so I just tried to tune it like a guitar, which mostly worked. I have a good ear, and as I listened to the songs, I could tell that the bass mostly played one note at a time, so I was able to fumble my way through the songs well enough that the guys decided to let me in their band. I think they really decided when they heard me sing, and when they heard me say "Sure, I can buy a PA system!" As I said, I really wanted to be in a band, and at that point I was not above buying my way in. So, I went to my grandmother and talked her into co-signing a loan, so I could buy a PA system, and I was in!

We worked hard and somehow, I got at least proficient enough on bass that I could play the songs we wanted to play and bought my own bass (a Gibson Grabber bass, because it looked like the bass that Gene Simmons used in Kiss) and amp. We started doing some local gigs and were considered pretty good in our little circle. So here is where things start getting interesting...

One of the guys in the band, Billy Peterson, and I became best friends. Billy had an older brother who was an MP in the Army, stationed at Fort Bliss, which is near El Paso, Texas. Billy was talking to his brother, who recommended that we go out to El Paso with our band to play, so of course that's what we did. A few details about the trip:

1. We did not have a gig in El Paso—we were going with the assumption that we would be able to procure one when we got there.

2. We had two vehicles capable of making the trip: my 1964 Ford pickup with the three-speed shifter on the column, a straight-six engine, and no air conditioning. The other vehicle was an early 70's station wagon, also with no air conditioning.

3. We had to rent a U-Haul trailer to put our equipment in and pull it behind the pickup. This meant that I had to get some welding done underneath the truck, or my dad was not going to let me go.

4. We were a bunch of stupid teenagers.

Number four was probably the most significant detail about this trip and was the reason for one through three. Nevertheless, we somehow got it together enough to prepare for our trip, which was to occur in the summer. That is an important detail. On the day before our trip was to commence, I went to the local U-Haul location and rented a trailer; the U-Haul dude was very helpful, and I think a little envious of our pending journey, but unfortunately, he was apparently not very good at his job. As I drove away from the U-Haul site and got a couple hundred yards down the road, something caught my attention to my right. I looked out and saw a trailer rolling along on its own, aiming directly for some railroad tracks between two buildings. My first thought: "Well that's weird." My second thought, after looking in my rearview mirror: "Hey, where is my trailer?" My third thought, putting it all together: "*Hey, that's my trailer!*" I cringed as I watched the trailer careen between two buildings, narrowly missing both, and coming to rest against the railroad tracks. Obviously, the U-Haul dude did not attach it properly to the ball, and that's what happens when you don't attach your trailer securely to your ball. We retrieved the trailer, and soon were on our way south and then east toward El Paso.

It was very hot on the way to El Paso, and we drove most of the way at night. When we arrived, we met with Billy's brother, and his somewhat-less-than-happy-with-having-five-long-haired-teenagers-camping-out-at-their-two-bedroom-apartment wife, and immediately got the bright idea to go across the bridge into Juarez, Mexico. I think it would be somewhat risky to try going into Juarez these days, but back then it just seemed like some good fun. We arrived at the border, and walked across the bridge over the Rio Grande, which was actually not very grand at all; it was more or less a very wide ditch, with a little trickle of water flowing down the middle. I haven't been there in many years, so it may be different now, but at that time you would see dozens of little kids below in the empty river yelling "Penny! Penny!" Hoping that you would throw a little change to them from off the bridge, and the older and more enterprising kids would have a basket on the end of a long stick so that they could catch the change before anyone else got to it. Clever, but sad.

At any rate, we got to the other side of the bridge, and the first place we came to had a middle-aged man out front, saying "Come in, Yankee! Come in!" Of course, we all went in; I was not into drinking alcohol, but a beer sounded interesting to the rest of the group, so we shuffled through the darkened doorway. We emerged in an equally dark room, with about three tables and a circular stage offset to the right in front of us. Here is another really stupid note: we had used all of our money getting to El Paso. I was the only one with any money left, and that was a twenty-dollar bill, which was going to have to last us until we got a gig or starved to death, whichever came first. Our friend from the bar came to the table, the other four ordered beers, and I gave the man my twenty-dollar bill. I know you can see what's coming, but wait for it...

Our friend brought the warm beers, and about that time a woman came out of a door to the right of the stage. When telling this story, I have described her as looking like a jellybean with legs, but in honor of our friends south of the border, I am amending that to pinto bean; in either case you get the point that she was somewhat rotund. She also seemed to be about fifty years old, although she may just have been "rode hard and put away wet", as the saying goes. She was wearing a black negligee and panties, and black high heels that looked both too small and too old. At that moment our friend returned with a tray full of six shot glasses filled with an amber liquid, which he placed on a small table on the stage. Bean lady quickly downed all six shots; I didn't really know anything about that kind of alcohol at the time, but I thought, from her grimacing and shaking, that it must not taste too good.

Our friend left, and Bean lady went to the back of the stage, where an old record player sat on a small table and put on a scratchy song that sounded vaguely mariachi-like. Then, she began dancing around the stage. Actually, you couldn't strictly call it dancing; it looked more like organized stumbling. My bandmates seemed to find this tremendously amusing, but I remember feeling almost unbearably uncomfortable. Many a joke was being cracked at the table, including one of my bandmates asking her if she played the violin, which I did find humorous. Then, the coup de grace; in the midst of her gyrations, she began asking, in heavily accented English: "Okay, who wants to fuck? Who wants to fuck?" Well, this was too much for me. I went into the bathroom, just to the left of the room, and found that the lights were out; I fumbled for the light switch, and upon flipping it, saw thousands of cock roaches scattering in every direction. I jumped from being startled and revolted and bolted from the room. At this point it was clearly time to make our leave; I went to our friend from the bar and said, "We have to go. Can I get my change?"

Well, of course you know what's coming next. He smiled like a fox in a henhouse, and said, "Oh, no, Yankee, you got to pay for the entertainment." What was I to do? Argue or fight with the guy and get thrown in Mexican jail? The one and only smart move I made that day was slinking out the joint and back across the border as quickly as possible. *Sheesh!*

So, what happened? Did we end up starving? Not exactly...Billy's brother kept us floating for a few days by providing enough food for us to survive, and somehow, we finagled a showcase at one of the local clubs. The club wasn't interested in hiring us, but the owner of a rival club saw our showcase and hired us on the spot, and we ended up playing there for four weeks, making enough to survive on and enough to eventually get back home. I know, what a relief.

So where did I get hurt in all of this? For that part of the story, we need to go back to the beginning of the trip. Billy and I were riding in my pickup, pulling the U-Haul trailer, and we were approaching an area called The Grapevine; anyone from California will be familiar with this, but for those of you who are not, this is the path through the mountains just north of the Los Angeles area that leads into the massive San Joaquin Valley and central California. As mentioned, it was summer, and I thought I'd better stop and check the radiator of my old pickup, as we didn't want to take the chance of overheating on the climb up and over The Grapevine. I turned off the truck (which I later learned was a drastic mistake), got out, and opened the hood. When a car engine is running, the fluid is circulating throughout the engine, but when you turn off the engine, at least until the engine cools down, and extreme amount of pressure builds up. This tidbit of information would have been handy for me to know in advance of my next action. What I did was take off my shirt, as I at least had enough awareness to know that the radiator cap was hot, and I used it to insulate my hand from the cap as I turned it. The cap popped off like the lid of a pressure cooker, hitting me in the forehead, and I was doused with boiling water that came jetting out of the radiator. At the risk of criminal understatement, let me say that was a bummer.

There was a second or two when this happened that I didn't feel anything but wet, but very quickly I felt the burn, and not in a good, exercise video from the 80's kind of way. The left side of my face and body instantly turned red, as if I were a lobster that only got put half-way into the pot. Luckily, I didn't get much in the way of blisters, although the redness did last for a couple of weeks, and skin that sloughed off after that. At the time that it happened, Billy had a brief moment when I think he was concerned about me, and then a much longer moment in which he laughed until he peed his pants, and who could blame him.

What is the moral of this story? Listen, does every story have to have a moral? Can't stupidity be its own moral, at least once in a while? I submit that it can, and in this case is. I thank you.

The Melvyns Gang

I've been putting off writing this chapter. Mainly because, despite all the evidence presented in these stories, I don't really consider myself stupid; I have test scores to prove it, if you really want to know. When I was going through college, trying to decide on a major after several years of messing around, I thought it might be good to figure out what exactly was wrong with me. In physician heal thyself mode, I decided to major in psychology. I found it mostly interesting, but after graduating found that my only option, if I intended on any kind of gainful employment in a related field, was to continue my education. I decided that I would go for a Pupil Personnel Services credential, which would allow me to work as a school counselor. One of the courses required was Psychological Testing, in which you explore the various assessments commonly used, including a series of IQ tests. One of the assignments was to take the IQ tests, then write reflections on the outcome of the various assessments and interpret their meaning as if we were a client. Okay, this completely sounds like bragging, and in a way, I suppose it is, but in another, more significant way, it's a comment about self-worth; you'll see what I mean in a moment.

After summarizing the results of the various IQ tests and submitting the paper to my professor, his comment was that the profile of scores, and the insight of my responses, would indicate that I should strongly consider becoming a professor of Psychology. My thought upon reading that was that he needed to read it again, because there is no way I was smart enough for something like that. I know my scores were high, but that's only because the tests were easy, not because I'm smart. Look, I'll prove it by telling you the story of the Melvyn's gang; you will have to agree that this is not the behavior of a smart person, neither for participating nor for admitting to it. **Gulp**, here goes...

Ricky was ostensibly the leader of the Melvyn's gang, although there was no formal organization. He was a short, banty-rooster of a fellow, always with a big smile and a joke, but also ready to punch a guy in the face if provoked. He was an employee of Roller City, a Skate Guard, and he was pretty reliable and good at the job, as far as that went. His claim to fame, at least prior to the big Melvyns job, was that he could do a backflip on skates. Despite being rather social, he would tell me that his idea of a party was watching TV by himself with a box of cookies and a six pack of Pepsi.

Jerry was the youngest of the gang; he and Ricky were cousins and lived in the same house. Jerry was not an employee of the skating rink, but he was there every day. He was missing one of his ears from an accident as a small child and had a prosthetic ear that he would take off to freak out girls. He was the tallest of the group at five feet-nine inches and could accurately be described as wiry. He had the strange combination of being socially awkward and loquacious at the same time, and an utter lack of self-awareness that was simultaneously endearing and off-putting.

Jimmy was Jerry's older brother; a little shorter and more huskily built, he was also employed as a Skate Guard, although not as good at his job as Ricky. He was eventually let go, which led to all that follows. He had the same personal traits as Jerry which made them comical to be around, in the same way that you might get a kick out of watching a trained bear ride a bicycle, and much like the bear, if you turn your back, he might eat you for lunch. A good guy to have on your side, not a good guy to have against you.

Jughead was the wild card. Much older than the rest, he was a Vietnam vet with a face not even his mother could love. Huge buck teeth jutted out of his mouth, and an unruly shock of blond hair crowned his head. Only five feet five-inches tall, he was burly and stout from constant bodybuilding. He was quiet but friendly, but just under the surface you could see that, if he was not unhinged, then his hinge was being held in place by a very fine thread.

Because these fellows were at the rink every day, and because they were amusing in a reckless way, we became friends and I would hang out with them mainly while at work, but occasionally outside of work as well. I was on a completely different trajectory as all of them; I was a college student, and I don't think any of them, aside from Jughead, even graduated from high school. However, although we were on different life paths, we came from the same place; poor farmworkers were in all of our immediate backgrounds, so I suppose that shared history led to me feeling a certain kinship. Nevertheless, if you saw us together, it would be like the old Sesame Street game: "*One of these things is not like the others...*"

I was hurt in a severe emotional way as a result of my association with these guys, which I'll regretfully describe shortly, but I was also hurt physically on more than one occasion. Wait, here's one of those times now...

I was working as DJ, which I typically did, running the skating session, when I noticed Ricky being confronted by a guy much bigger than him. I should mention that Ricky considered himself a bit of a lothario, and had been flirting with this large fellow's girlfriend, leading to the confrontation. As previously described, Ricky was diminutive; stupidly, he was not afraid, but he was about to get pummeled. I quickly skated out to intercede, but before I got there another guy whom I didn't recognize got between them and began sticking up for Ricky. He and the larger guy began pushing one another, and then I got between them, telling them both to turn in their skates and leave the building. Problem solved, right?

They did both remove their skates, but then began fighting in the middle of the snack bar area, right in the middle of mothers and little kids in the midst of various birthday parties and etc. Now, here is where my reputation at Roller City was birthed, but I am here to tell you I both didn't mean for it to happen, and I got lucky (or unlucky, depending on your frame of reference). I knew I had to stop them from fighting; it both looked bad for the rink, and little kids nearby might have been hurt, so I skated up, jumped the waist-high wall, and got between the combatants. I was holding them apart, looking at the bigger of the two, who was several inches taller than me, when the one behind me took a swing and hit me in the back of the head. I don't think he was trying to hit me, and I hadn't planned on doing it, but in a flash reaction I spun and hit him square in the nose, knocking him flat on his back and causing an immediate spray of blood to fly from his face. I want to make it clear that I didn't mean to do this, and I regret it; I am not a violent person in general, and I am not proud of having hit someone in this manner. However, although it was mainly an accident, the results were very impressive. He was out cold, lying flat on his back covered with blood. I could feel the bigger guy pushing against me, trying to get at the now prone co-combatant, and in an instinctive reaction I turned and shoved him in his chest, causing him to fall backwards; he hit the back of his head on the edge of a picnic table and fell to the ground, stunned and now totally compliant.

To any witnesses of this encounter, it looked like I had just taken out two rather large guys in the space of three seconds, which is literally what happened. However, I didn't intend to do any of it. I didn't know what to do at that point; I was completely panicked and skated off to the office to find the manager to tell him what had occurred. His reaction was unexpected; he laughed and said "Just stay here out of sight. I'll take care of it." I looked down at my left hand, which was now throbbing. I had hit the first fighter so hard that the fingernail on my middle finger split all the way down to the quick, and it ached. He ran the fighters off; I thought for sure that I would be arrested for assault, but no one called the police; I thought for sure these guys would return with guns or groups of gang-members to get me, but they never came back. Somehow, I escaped with nothing more than a mangled finger, and there is a crease in my fingernail from the split that occurred that is still there today.

Although utterly undeserved, I now had a reputation, as you might imagine: "Don't mess with that guy, he'll knock you out!" I would be lying if I said that I didn't get just a little bit of pleasure out of this at the time, though, despite that reputation being undeserved. You are much more likely to find me quietly reading a book than getting involved in a dustup.

The rest of this story does not involve physical injury, at least not for me, but it does involve some rather deep emotional injury and led to me changing my life drastically. Ricky had developed a rivalry with another of the lowlifes that frequented the skating rink, who we'll call Jabrony, and they made plans to fight in front of the Jack In The Box restaurant on the main street in town, a totally classy move. Of course, all the Melvyns gang went along for "emotional support", and I tagged along to see if I could get a good laugh out of the proceedings. It was assumed that Jabrony would have a similar emotional support group, and he did not disappoint; he had actually assembled a larger group than Ricky, including one rather mountainous fellow whom I had never seen before. As Ricky approached Jabrony, it was clear that Mountain Man was planning on interceding, but they were not accounting for the wild card, Jughead. Jughead approached at a sprint, and Mountain Man did not see him coming; he leaped, and snared

Mountain Man in a choke hold, taking him to the ground and squeezing his neck so tightly that Mountain Man very quickly became unconscious. Jabrony was not a fighter, and after two or three punches from Ricky, he fell to the ground, asking for mercy. At that moment I could hear sirens wailing; it was clear that the police had been alerted, and equally clear that we needed to quickly vacate the premises.

We hopped into our vehicles and went to a nearby apartment complex, which was not euphemistically at all called Sin City. People in Section 8 housing looked down on this area, that's how monumentally crappy it was. The Melvynites had a cousin who lived there, Nimrod, and we all piled into his apartment, laughing and carrying on about current events. Nimrod was different from the rest of the Melvynites; taller and darker in terms of temperament. Where they appeared carefree and happy-go-lucky, he appeared dangerous and slightly unstable; there was something abnormal in the eyes that gave it away. Nevertheless, there we were, yucking it up, until there was a vicious pounding at the door, and angry voices shouting, "*Open the fuckin' door, asshole!*" and various other, equally eloquent rejoinders. A peek out the window into the Sin City night revealed approximately twenty seemingly unhappy chaps. Let me ask you this: why is it that males feel the need to remove their shirts when worked up into an angry frenzy? Whatever the reason, many of these scholars had done so, most with less-than-impressive results. Nevertheless, we were outnumbered at least four-to-one, and many of those outside demanding to enter were carrying weapons of various kinds: baseball bats and the like.

We ran around the apartment in a panic, looking for nonexistent places to hide, while Nimrod calmly walked into his bedroom. He returned with something in his hand and approached the door. Upon closer inspection, I saw that it was a handgun of some kind; I should note that I don't like guns and have no experience with them, and I suddenly was more afraid of Nimrod than of the crowd outside. Nimrod flung the door open, shouting "*Back off, dickheads!*" and holding the gun in front of him with both hands, his arms outstretched. This led to a very rapid scattering of the mob outside, and an equally rapid exodus from Sin City by the Melvynites. I was too petrified to move, but after a minute or so, Nimrod said, "You better take off—they'll probably come back." I didn't need any other prompting; I ran from the apartment, found my car, sped home, jumped into bed and hid under the covers. *How did I get involved in this mess? And more importantly, how am I going to get out of it without getting killed or thrown in jail*? Here is what I did: the following day, I began packing, and within a week I moved to the town where I was attending college. Up to that time I had been commuting, and I never saw the Melvynites again. Now, the rest of their story...

By now Jimmy had been let go by Roller City, and eventually was able to land a job at Melvyns. Some of you may not be familiar with Melvyns—they have been out of business for several years, but at one time had a chain of mid-scale department stores, perhaps most comparable to JC Penney. Jimmy was working there for a few months and had been taking note of when cash was gathered and taken to the vault, for later transfer to armored truck. He and the other Melvynites hatched a plan to steal the money as it was being transferred to the vault by doing a grab-and-run style activity. On the day in question, as the money was being transferred three of the Melvynites entered the store with handkerchiefs tied over their faces while Jughead waited outside in the escape vehicle. I know, seems like a bad scene in an action movie, in which the faceless criminals are taken down in the midst of their nefarious act by Sylvester Stallone while wearing cowboy boots and sunglasses, and after pummeling them, he would say, "Yo, welcome to Melvyns. Have a nice day," or something to that effect.

Unfortunately, that's not what happened. What did happen was that they were able to snatch the money bag out of the hand of the female assistant manager, and ran for the door, with a security guard in pursuit. They burst out of the glass doors and ran for the car, and it must have been that they were not going to be able to make it before the security guard got to them; whatever the case, Jughead leaned out of the car window and shot the security guard. Luckily, he was not killed, but I don't need to tell you, friends, that shooting the security guard is not good. Of course, the police were already on their way, and the Melvyns Gang was caught before they even got out of the parking lot. All were convicted and spent significant time in prison; some of them may still be incarcerated for all I know.

And this is the group I was hanging out with, albeit for that thankfully brief period of time. As you can imagine, this led to some extended reflection and soul-searching, and to the cancellation of my Melvyns credit card.

What is the moral of this story? Gun safety and electronic money transfers—'nuff said.

Stop That Biting, Eugene

I have had a long and sort of meandering work career, at least in part because I really just wanted to be a musician. The problem I had as a musician was that I didn't have it in me to self-promote so I was not able to make it a career long-term. I have had lots of notable experiences in the workplace, and maybe I'll put those in writing at some later time.

My work history includes a stint with the County Probation Department, and that's where the next story comes in. I worked as a Probation Officer for four years. This is something I really had no interest in—in fact I didn't even know what a Probation Officer did before applying. I just knew that it paid better than the psych hospital where I was working at the time, and I had a friend who worked there and told me of an opening. I applied and obviously they hired me, or I wouldn't be writing about it, now would I?

I was a juvenile investigating officer for the probation department, which meant that, after the court had decided the juvenile had committed the crime, I would talk to the juvenile, the parents, and victims if there were any, and then make a recommendation to the court as to what the punishment for the crime ought to be. I had many, many bizarre experiences going into people's homes to do my investigations, but this one is the only one in which I was physically hurt...

The juvenile in question had committed the crime of theft. Who did he steal from? His grandmother. She had been squirreling away money her whole life and had amassed seventeen thousand bucks. However, instead of keeping it in a bank, she kept it all in a cabinet in the family's four-hundred-dollar-per-month apartment in the worst part of the worst town in the county. He found the money, took it all, bought a stolen ATV, and blew the rest on drugs. What a prince.

On the day in question, I arrived at their apartment and had to work up a little nerve to get out and approach the door. The area did not give one the feeling of safety, to state it mildly. I walked past the trash- and weed-infested yard and knocked on the door. After a moment, the juvenile's mother answered the door. She was approximately five feet tall, and approximately five feet wide, was wearing a massively stressed tank top, stretched to the very limits of its tensile strength, and did not appear to be wearing the usual undergarments that a woman of such stature might wear. She also appeared to be allergic to teeth, as most had vacated the premises. "Well, come on in," she drawled; I looked down and saw that virtually every square inch of the floor of the tiny living room was covered in trash: fast food wrappers, cups, and similar items. I trudged into the room, and she continued, "Well, Junior's not here right now, not sure where he's got to, and grannie's not here neither. You want I should brang Junior's daddy out?"

"Uh, sure," I ventured, "I need to hear from all of you, so I can make a recommendation to the court about what we should do with...Junior, I guess."

"Well, have a sit down on that couch right there and I'll fetch 'im." I looked around and noted that there were two dilapidated couches in the room, but no other furniture. The doorway to the hall and presumably a bedroom or two was to the left, so I sat on the couch on the right. As I sat, I noticed that something appeared to be moving, then noticed that I was covered with *fleas*. I leapt up from the couch almost involuntarily, brushed myself off and remained standing until mom and dad returned.

"Well go ahead and sit down, honey," said mom.

"Uh, I'm okay, I've, ah, I've been sitting in the car all day," I lied.

"Well suit yerself. Say hi, dad." Dad did not say hi. In fact, he didn't say anything; he shuffled into the room and sat on the opposing couch, looking down, mouth agape. I noticed a little bit of drool coming out, and, looking closer, saw what looked like small holes that had been drilled on both sides of his head. He never said a word, never looked up, and mom never said anything else to him, so I never discovered what his malady was, although based on appearance I would say he had either had a broken neck, a lobotomy, or both.

I then heard a rustling sound to my right; I looked over and saw a tiny kitchenette, closed off by a baby fence, and behind the fence in the kitchenette were three mangy dogs. One was missing an ear, and another only had three legs. About this time, I was wondering if I had entered an alternate universe or some sort of rift in the time-space continuum. "I'm not sure when we'll see Junior, but he done a real bad thang, takin' his grannie's cash like that," mom offered, in a rather gross understatement. It became clear she was trying to entertain me when she said, "Hey, you wanna see our iguana?"

"Well, ah, sure," I lied again; all I really wanted was to leave as quickly as possible, take a shower, and burn my clothes. Mom left but returned quickly with a medium-sized iguana in hand. She held it in front of her saying, "See? His name's Eugene!" except that she accented the first syllable, as in YOU-gene.

Continuing to try to be nice, I said, "Well, look at that!" and extended my finger as if to pet its head. Unfortunately for me, YOU-gene had different ideas. He bolted from mom's hand and latched on to the end of my index finger, sinking in his little teeth and dangling there.

Said mom, "Oh, sorry 'bout that. You stop that biting, YOU-gene!" and she pried him off my finger, now dripping blood on the trash-covered floor.

"Well, will you look at that!" said mom. "Here, let me git that!" and she held out the bottom of her tank top, as if to have me wipe my bloody finger on her shirt.

I had finally reached my limit. "No, no, that's okay," I said, "I better get going. Why don't you just call me when Junior gets in."

Mom looked a little disappointed; I think she liked my company. "Well okay, honey, if you say so. Sorry you wasted a trip!" While standing and preparing to leave, I noticed what looked like a small, stuffed bird sitting on the top of dad's couch. As I turned to leave, the bird moved, which startled me a bit. Mom noticed, and said, "Oh, how do you like little Owley? We found him outside. He only gots one leg!" Sure enough, as I looked closer, I could see that it was a live baby owl, and it did indeed only gots one leg, sitting out in the open on the back of the flea-ridden couch.

I remember seeing a terrible horror movie long ago entitled C.H.U.D., which stood for Cannibalistic Humanoid Underground Dwellers. While standing there, it occurred to me that perhaps it was less of a movie and more of a documentary. "Oh, oh, okay, thanks folks, see you in court," I said on my way out the door. I ran to my car, drove to a safer part of town, stopped, and cried for fifteen minutes. Okay, I didn't really do that, but I kind of felt like it.

Did you know that lizards tend to carry some nasty bacteria in their mouths? I got a pretty bad infection from YOU-gene. So, what happened to Junior? Not sure, he didn't show up to court. I recommended that he be placed in the Juvenile Detention Facility Boot

Camp, and that he pays restitution to grannie, but if he lives to be a thousand he would be unlikely to pay her back.

So, what is the moral of this story? Stay in school, kids, and study science. Science is the only thing that will save us when the C.H.U.D. uprising comes, and it's coming *soon*.

Getting Un-Stoned

People have colloquial cures for almost any kind of ailment or injury, and often they are different based on region, culture, or both. Here in the western world, we like to think that our method of addressing ailments or injuries is science-based, and in many instances it is. However, at the street, or maybe more specifically home level, things can get downright strange. I once witnessed a Hispanic lady pass out, and her family was all around her; an older gentleman who was with the group lit up a cigarette and began blowing the smoke into her face to revive her. I guess there is some logic in that, but it just seemed very strange to me. It seemed to work, though, as she started coughing and eventually came to.

When I was a young boy, maybe eight or nine, I don't know why I did this, but I went to bed with my shoes on. Maybe I was planning on sleepwalking, I don't know. At any rate, when I woke up in the morning, for some reason my feet had swollen to about twice their normal size, and I had a very difficult time getting my shoes off. I showed my parents and they had me soak my feet in a combination of cigarette tobacco and warm water. I was too young and inexperienced at that time to think this was really weird, but if someone suggested doing that today I would probably refuse to do it.

What is one of the more common colloquial treatments for heartburn? I had always heard that if you have heartburn, drinking a glass of milk would help. I suppose the thought was that it would coat your innards or something. At any rate, it may work for heartburn, but...

To set the scene, let me say that for most of my life I was addicted to sugar and fat, although I have been off the sugar for a number of years. Like any addict, though, I am only one slip away from falling off the wagon...I know, "Oh, wow, you're really *hard core*." What can I say, those were my drugs of choice. Donuts, cake, cookies, pie, pastries—the quality did not matter to any appreciable degree. When that is what you eat for the majority of your diet for long periods of time, even if you are able to avoid becoming fat, it still has some other, shall we say, undesired effects on your body. They may take years to surface, but surface they will. Now, to the story.

During my years as a high school counselor, I was the advisor for our Asian Club on campus, and on the day in question, it was International Food Day; the various clubs and groups on campus would bring food items from around the world and sell them at lunch. The parents of a couple of my students had a restaurant and brought in the big wok assembly to make fried egg rolls. Fried egg rolls are one of the more delicious treats, and I treated myself to about 12 of them. I would occasionally need to work into the evening, as I did on International Foods Day. In the afternoon, I began experiencing what I assumed was heartburn; although I thought the egg rolls were tasty, my stomach did not seem to agree. Finally, at about six pm, I decided that I would try the aforementioned colloquial treatment. I left, thinking that I would stop at a convenience store or the like, but then saw, like a beacon on a hill, like a lighthouse in the dark of night, the mecca, the high-water mark for all fast food, Jack in the Box. My thought: "At least I won't have to get out of the car." I pulled into the drive thru and spoke into Jack's smiling face: "Do you have any milk?"

After the drive thru girl stopped snickering, she said, "We don't got any milk. You could get a milkshake." Well, if milk is good for heartburn, a milkshake must be even better, right? I ordered up a vanilla shake (it looks the most like milk) and drank it on my way back to work.

I continued to work, but now the heartburn was becoming unbearable, and I was beginning to think that I was having a heart attack. So, I went to my favorite haunt, the emergency room; did you know if you are a vaguely middle-aged man with chest pain, they will take you in right away, no waiting? I didn't but I do now. They whisked me in and hooked me up to what seemed like every machine in the hospital, and eventually the doctor came in. After looking through the data that had been collected, he said, "Well, you are not having a heart attack. There's nothing wrong with your heart. What you are having is a gall bladder attack. Did you eat something high in fat today?" Hmmm, let me see—you mean like 12 deep fried egg rolls and a vanilla milkshake?

Did you know that the gall bladder is responsible for producing bile, which funnels into the stomach to help break down food, and that fat in food is one of the things that cause the gall bladder to have to work extra hard? I didn't know any of that—I didn't even know what a gall bladder was before this incident. I know now, in intimate detail. My gall bladder was working like an orchard full of field workers getting paid by the box and was still unable to keep up with the amount of bile needed, because it was packed full of gall stones. I know this because I had to have my gall bladder removed due to it being packed full of gall stones. Luckily for me, it's a pretty simple surgery nowadays, only requiring a couple of small incisions. Did you know that other areas of the body also produce bile, so you don't really need your gall bladder? I know, as my friends in the rap community might say, I'm droppin some knowledge on ya, *boieee.*

After surgery, I was given a bag containing the gall stones, and it looked like a bag full of milk duds of various sizes, although I don't think you would want to pop any of these into your mouth. I still have the stones; I'm thinking about getting them made into a necklace, kind of like puca shells, but round and brown, which is really not much like puca shells at all, come to think of it. They might have a smell to them, too, which might not be great for a necklace. Okay, scratch the necklace idea, that was dumb.

The moral of this story? It's two-fold: whether you are eating your dinner or eating your feelings, try to knock off the sugar content—you'll thank me in the long run. And, as far as jewelry is concerned, stick to the classic styles; they never go out of fashion. You're welcome!

Ladies and Gentlemen, Please Welcome Once Again, The Stones—No, Not Those Old Dudes

The first time I had a kidney stone I thought one of my internal organs had burst. Yeah, I know, I had gall stones, now kidney stones. I'm trying to corner the stone market, okay? I was awakened at three in the morning by this horrible pain for which I had no frame of reference. I knew nothing about kidney stones, and frankly for a few moments I thought, 'This is it. After all the crap I've done and been through, to be taken down this way seems a bit anti-climactic.'

I'm not at all exaggerating when I describe any of this. Kidney stones are a stone-cold bummer, friend. I know women who have had both children and kidney stones, and they tell me the kidney stone was worse. I'll never know, so I'll have to take their word for it; all I can tell you is the only position I could get any relief at all from the pain was on my hands and knees, rocking back and forth. If I had been watching myself as that was happening, I'm pretty sure I would have been amused by this person moaning and rocking, looking suspiciously like he was having sex with a ghost. After about an hour of this, and fearing for my life, I went to the ER, my old stomping grounds. Just as before, after a series of tests and beeping machines, the doctor told me that I was probably not dying, and explained to me how kidney stones work, although to be honest I tuned out after the not dying part.

Eventually the pain subsided, although it returned periodically over the next couple of weeks (yes, weeks; this first stone was rather stubborn), along with an uncontrollable urge to empty an already empty bladder.

As you can imagine, it's a bit frustrating, not to mention painful, to stand there (or sit there, as the case may be) for twenty minutes trying in vain to get at least a drop to come out.

Finally, on a Sunday, I was at church when the urge to pee hit me. I went into the restroom and stood there in a stall, gazing up at the ceiling, thinking, 'Oh, come on, just a drop, that's all I'm asking.' After a few minutes, and totally without feeling anything, er, *making its egress* from that most sensitive of passageways, I heard a seductive *plink!* I gazed into the porcelain waters, and there, settling into the bottom, was... a smooth stone about the size of a tiny pebble, or maybe a large grain of sand. What a ripoff! All that pain, all that anguish and turmoil for *that?* I'm gonna... I'm gonna talk to the manager, that's what I'm gonna do. I demand satisfaction!

Eventually, I went to a specialist who took an MRI of my kidneys, and found a number of small stones floating around, just waiting their turn to torture me. He said the small ones are the worst, because they are the ones that you end up passing, and in the succeeding years I've passed several of them, mostly in a day or two instead of weeks, although on one other occasion I had an attack that would not stop. After four hours of simulated ghost sex, I went back to the ER, where by this time we were on a first-name basis. They took me into a room, where I sat (or ghost sexed, punctuated by failed attempts to pee) for four more hours before the doctor finally came in. Forty-five minutes later, a nurse entered and gave me a morphine shot in the middle of my back. If you've ever had a morphine shot, you know what that experience is like, but if not, let me tell you, the effect is immediate. From the chest down it felt like my body was on fire, but there was no pain; it's easy to see how people get addicted to that stuff.

Now, to the story. My band was scheduled to play at a large Halloween function, and we had to travel sixty miles or so to the venue to set up.

On the way there, I began experiencing a by-now familiar introduction to the kidney stone opera, and by the time we were done with set up and waiting to go onstage, I was in defcon one (a little edumacation for ya: the military defcon levels go in reverse order, so defcon one is the highest level. You're welcome!) I was ghost sexing in a two-foot gap from the back of the stage to the rear wall of the facility, doing my best not to moan too loudly, although it probably would have added to the ambiance, it being a Halloween gig. The attack waned by the time we went on stage, and I soldiered through the gig, sweating and running to the bathroom to not pee between every set. It was a freakin' bummer, friend.

At the end of the night, as we were packing up our equipment, I felt a pain in my, shall we say, *exit tunnel*, which was decidedly unwelcome. I dashed to the bathroom, where, once in the stall, gazed at said tunnel, and saw a small lump where one should not be. With a herculean push of my bladder, I expelled the offending object, which turned into one of the funniest things I have ever witnessed; the flat, jagged item shot out like the world's smallest ninja throwing star, hovering frisbee-like for a moment before falling to its doom in the swirling waters. I sat down and laughed for about five minutes, although I could not say whether out of amusement or relief. I've passed several more kidney stones since then, but none as memorable.

And what is the moral to this sordid tale? Beware the ninja throwing star! Oh, and water. Drink lots of water.

Poop Tales

If you are squeamish about bodily functions, these next tales are not for you. But look, there is a tremendous amount of humor in these functions for precisely that reason. Why do we laugh when someone farts? It's just innately funny that this braying noise, and the corresponding cloud of noxious gas, comes out of our butts. Of course, not so funny when your big brother does it under the covers and then sticks your head under there, in a rendition of the infamous Dutch Oven, but hilarious when it happens to someone else, which is the very definition of schadenfreude. I would encourage you to get over yourself and read on; what, are you trying to tell me you never poop, or if you do it doesn't smell? *Liar!*

With that out of the way, let's get to the less delicate items. Namely, my bowels and other attached paraphernalia. We have always had a love-hate relationship, my bowels and I. I was once told by someone with an underdeveloped sense of humor that I was overly in touch with my alligator brain, and she didn't mean it as a joke, she meant it to be shaming, and I am repeating it here, so mission accomplished, little miss I-never-poop-and-if-I-do-it-doesn't-stink-and-I-don't-enjoy-it-anyway. The thing is, my bowels are poor communicators; I don't always get sufficient notice of their intentions, and at times the communication is rather insistent and urgent. It is painful in many ways, both before and during, and sometimes after, as in the following...

I have two daughters two years apart in age. When the oldest was five, we got her involved in various sports activities, including soccer, which at that age consists mainly of most of the kids on both teams surrounding the ball and following it from one end of the field to the other in a cloud of shuffling, cleated feet and tiny knee pads, with a few stragglers wandering around crying because they are tired or hungry or because the other kids won't play with them. The games (Matches? Contests? I don't know what they call them, but I do know that one of my bosses, a principal who was a crusty former football coach, called soccer *communist kickball*) occurred on an elementary school field. There would typically be four or five games going at the same time, and my daughter's game happened to be on the field furthest away from the elementary school buildings, which also meant it was the furthest away from any restrooms, which is an important detail. My daughter was in amongst the cloud of kicking youngsters when I began to feel a certain urge, which quickly became an indomitable command from my bowels to expunge their contents immediately if not sooner.

I was the only one related to my daughter at the communist kickball game, and I knew she might become frightened if I disappeared from the sidelines, but I was in a severe state, and something had to give. I had no choice, I had to make a run for it, hope she didn't notice, and get back quickly. I turned and began sprinting for the restroom, which was about a hundred yards away, and quickly realized that I was going to have extreme difficulty making it without incident. I burst through the doors, and luckily no one was in the restroom at that moment, because as I approached the stall, well, this is very uncomfortable to say, a few *items* were dropped on the floor. I couldn't worry about that at that moment, I needed to worry about taking care of the rest of the *items* first. Oh, did I mention that I was wearing gym shorts? I began cleaning myself as best I could, but of course the underwear had to go, which left me with only a pair of gym shorts between me and nudity, in front of hundreds of five-year-old communist kickball players and their parents.

As I was working out a way to clean myself, two kids entered the restroom. From their voices, I would judge them to be about ten or eleven years of age; I quickly pulled my legs up so as to make it appear that there was no one in the stall, and one of the youngsters shouted, "Oh, look! Someone *shit on the floor!* Oh, *gross!*" They quickly turned and bolted from the restroom, presumably to go find their parents to report the spillage, and I imagined them barging into the restroom, finding me there, and demanding my arrest for violation of penal code 221913292.77—Public Shittery. I bolted from the restroom about ten seconds after the two traumatized pre-teens and ran for my car. I lived nearby, and judged that I could make it home, change, and get back to the communist kickball game within five minutes if I sped and ignored such trivialities as stop signs and stop lights.

Four minutes later, I returned to the elementary school, dressed in different gym shorts and underwear, and jogged to the far field where my daughter was playing. She never even noticed I was gone.

WHILE WORKING AS A high school administrator, I had the opportunity on occasion to take groups of students on different field trips. On the day in question, I was to supervise a group of about thirty students to a student conference in a city about seventy miles away, which on a school bus is about a ninety-minute trip each way. We loaded the bus and began the trip unremarkably; however, about forty-five minutes down the road, I began to experience a familiar rumbling. *Let's see...half-way there, forty-five minutes to go...I think I can make it...* Unfortunately, that was very much wishful thinking. We still had about fifteen minutes to go, and my insides had ceased knocking and had now become a rampaging horde, doing their best to storm the castle walls. I was beginning to sweat and was working very hard to hold it together; I shuffled up to the bus driver and whispered, "Hey man, I need you to stop somewhere, or we are going to have a big problem if you know what I mean."

He looked at me and I could tell he knew what I meant. "Well," he said, "We'll be at the school where the conference is taking place in five minutes or so." Okay, I think I can wait five minutes...

Ten minutes later we pulled up to the school, and I was in an utter state of panic. I bolted from the bus, leaving the students behind, and ran up to a table set up in front of the gym, being staffed by two women sitting in folding chairs and presenting a vaguely teacher-like image. I quickly barged to the front of the line queuing up in front of them, and, cupping my hand around the side of my mouth in the manner you would use when you want to screen out people in the vicinity, but you want the person in front of you to hear explicitly, and hissed, "Sorry to cut, but could you tell me where the bathrooms are? This is an *emergency*."

As I stood, shifting from one leg to the other frantically, she put her finger to her lips in a thoughtful pose, and said, "You know, I don't think there is a bathroom in the gym. Do you know where the bathroom is, Bernice?"

Oh, crap, come on girls, things are about to get very messy. Said Bernice: "Well, let's see...I'm not sure, but I think there is one behind the gym, on the opposite side from where we are." At that I turned and bolted, sprinting for the opposite side of the gym. *It had to be on the opposite side...it just couldn't possibly be close by, could it? Did a sadist design this school?* My gait would have looked rather comical had anyone been around to see it, running as fast as I could while simultaneously squeezing my butt cheeks together tight enough to make a diamond out of a lump of coal. Luckily, there was no one around as I sped to the opposite side of the gym, and equally luckily, there was no one in the bathroom when I arrived. I burst through the doors and headed for a stall, but...look, there's no other way to say it; the *dirty deed* had already taken place. What am I going to do now? I'm here at a high school gym for six hours with hundreds of students from high schools throughout the area, I have a brown streak a foot long on the back of my pants, and I'm wearing *khakis!* To compound matters, as if they needed further compounding, this was a new high school, and in a well-intended effort to lower their waste, there were no paper towel dispensers in the restroom, only air hand dryers. I give the school an A for their environmental efforts, but an F- for sensitivity to those whose bowels are differently able (the folks in the field of special education will be laughing riotously at that joke, I think).

I spent the next ten minutes cleaning myself up as best I could, splashing myself with water from the toilet, as I thought it too risky to go out of the stall with no pants on. There was no hope for my underwear, though; they had to be disposed of. Remember the part about there being no paper towel dispensers in the bathroom? No paper towel dispensers, no need for a trashcan in which to dispose of paper towels. That's right, there was no trashcan in the bathroom. Miraculously, no one came into the bathroom the whole time I spent in there setting up shop, so I put my khakis back on, sans underwear, and poked my head out the door to see if anyone was around, soiled wad of boxers in hand. There was a row of low shrubs just outside the bathroom door, which seemed like as good a place as any, so I stashed the underwear underneath the shrubs and walked back around to the front of the gym. I had cleaned out my pants as best I could, but there was still a rather evident stain at the back, so as I slunk into the gym, I scooted along with my back to the wall and stayed standing with my back to the wall for the remainder of the *six-hour conference*. I'm quite sure that the students wondered why I was acting so strangely and why I was refusing to participate in any of the activities that were taking place, and why I did a weird sideways-walk thing to the bus as we were leaving, and why I waited until everyone had exited the bus when we arrived back at our home school, but they will never know, unless they read this of course.

What is the moral of this story? It's hard to overemphasize the importance of proper nutrition. Look, if your diet consists solely of fast food and diet cola, you are going to have some problems, dude.

Ricky, the Stoner Skateboarder

When you reach a certain, shall we say, *vintage*, things begin happening, seemingly of their own accord. For me, it was hypertension, among other things. It was noticed at a routine visit to the doctor, and at the next visit it was more elevated yet, so the doctor decided that I needed to be on medication. Here is where things start getting juicy.

As you would probably want, I was started on a fairly low dose of a medication that apparently was designed to make friends with the high blood pressure—sort of like keeping a terrorist from blowing up your house by being nice. At any rate, one morning I was busy at work when I began feeling a headache coming on, and, knowing that headaches can be one of the symptoms of a spike in blood pressure, I went to the school nurse (I probably did not mention that I am a high school administrator, providing me with the luxury of having a nurse nearby at all times). She welcomed me into her office, replete with posters of the kinds of effects that smoking, drinking, or illegal drugs have on your body (shriveling testicles is a student favorite) and checked my blood pressure. Then she checked it again. She then directed me to go to either my doctor or the emergency room, and she was by God going to make sure I did one of those two things. She also wouldn't let me drive myself; I think she wanted to call an ambulance, but I got one of my co-administrators to drive me to the doctor's office. When I left the school, my blood pressure was 165 over 115, and when I got to the doctor's office, it was 180 over 125. I have since come to know, based on their reaction to those numbers, that that is not good.

The doctor gave me two options: go to the emergency room by ambulance or get someone to take me there directly. I contacted my wife, who came quickly to pick me up; we have a way of reacting to these kinds of situations by joking our way through the whole thing, which is what we did. I guess that's as good an adaptive behavior as any, and it does tend to relieve stress, although when we arrived at the emergency room, they took me in directly and checked my blood pressure again, and this time it was 210 over 155—so much for the healing power of humor. The doctor on call came in rather quickly, and after looking at the chart said in a rather chipper tone, with a smile painted on his face, "Well, I think you are probably having a stroke! We're going to give you some medications and run some tests, so hang tight!"

Now, those are words that no one wants to hear, but I guess he thought it would lessen the blow if he delivered the news in an enthusiastic way. I responded by immediately beginning to wiggle my fingers and toes, noting that everything seemed to be working. My wife responded by saying, "Do you think we could hurry this up? I have some things to do." Okay, she didn't really say that, but I think it would have been hilarious if she had. Anyway, to make this portion of the story shorter, I was placed in the MRI machine, which showed that I did not have a stroke, and eventually was allowed to go home.

Needless to say, the doctor decided that I needed a more substantial dose of medication, so it was doubled. Yes, you guessed it, then the medication worked too well. Within a week or two I was feeling dizzy from the lowered blood pressure, but I assumed that was just how it worked, so I didn't really think too much about it. Now, I should note that my high blood pressure is hereditary; I am not significantly overweight, and I am somewhat compulsive about exercising regularly. So, one evening after being on the double helping of meds for a month or two, I was at the gym doing my thing, which usually includes a few miles of running on the treadmill and a little time in the sauna. Call me weird, I just like to sweat everything out before leaving the gym.

I had completed my exercises and went into the sauna, and finding it completely full of other patrons at various stages in their fitness journey (one unfortunate gentleman who spends lots of time in the sauna has a striking resemblance to Jabba the Hut), I stood against the wall of the sauna waiting for someone to leave so that I could have the joy of sitting in someone else's butt sweat. After about ten minutes, I was getting tired of standing, so I squatted down with my back against the wall and continued to wait for a seat.

Fifteen minutes later, there was still no available bench space, so I rose to exit the sauna. Now things got really interesting. As you may have experienced in your own life, if you squat down for an extended period of time, say fifteen minutes, and then rise quickly, you may feel a little lightheaded, or even dizzy. When you are on a double helping of high blood pressure meds, that sensation is, shall we say, greatly amplified. I was only a step away from the door, and as I pushed it open, I remember thinking "*Uh-oh.*" Not very eloquent, but I didn't have time for anything else, as I passed out, falling like a plank on my face. I was out so completely that I dreamed in the minute or so that I was unconscious; my dream included a beach scene, and I assume that is because the exit from the sauna looks out onto a large indoor pool area which includes a lap pool to the right and two smaller, Jacuzzi-style pools to the left. I fell onto the concrete pool decking, and when I came to, I was very confused. Someone was shoving a towel onto my face, and telling to hold still, although I couldn't in that moment understand why; apparently, I may have convulsed a little after falling, and the other patrons were rather concerned. I noticed that the towel against my face was covered in blood, and it was running down my right arm, dripping onto my sweat-soaked shorts.

"Hold still," a woman's voice said in my ear, "we thought you were *dead.*"

I thought of all the pithy quips I could have made, but all I said was "Okay." As I sat on the pool deck, my back against the wall, the blood-soaked towel jammed up against my face, I noticed a man lying next to the Jacuzzi pool at the far end of the large room; he was approximately thirty yards away, but I could see clearly that his legs were blue, which I decided was likely not a good sign. The gym had officially become a treacherous place.

At that moment, EMTs arrived with a stretcher; they approached me, but I said, "I'm okay, go get that guy over there. I think he's dead." They did so, rather quickly, and as they did, I got out my cell phone and called my wife. Here is how that conversation went:

Her: "Hello?"

Me: "Hey, what are you doing?"

Her: "I'm just over here working like always. Let me tell you, my kids were terrible today (I should have mentioned my wife is a second-grade teacher, and a great one), I think Juanito needs to be tested for special ed. Either that or he needs some medication or new parents or both."

Me: "You probably need to refer him to the School Psych for assessment."

Her: "Well duh. I already did. Why did you call?"

Me: "Oh, I'm just over here at the gym, and I kind of fell down."

Her: "Well are you okay?"

Me: "Well, I kind of cut myself when I fell, and do you think you could come by and pick me up and take me to the emergency room?"

Her: "*WHAT?!! Why didn't you say something when I first answered?!*"

Me: "Well, I don't know, it seemed like you had something to say."

Her: "You are an idiot. I'll be there in a minute."

Okay, I'm not sure she called me an idiot, but it would have been funnier if she had. She arrived quickly and seeing all the blood on the towel and on my arm and shorts, realized that I was indeed an idiot. I slunk out to the car, and we quickly found ourselves in the emergency room once again. As I was covered in blood, they took me in immediately; I had a gaping hole about two inches across in my cheek where a chunk of flesh had been torn away by my fall onto the pool deck, plus a couple of other smaller scrapes. As my injury was not life-threatening, I was told to sit in the last of a row of chairs with other patients with various ailments and complaints.

I sat for a moment, and then heard, from the examining room directly in front of me: "Ow. Owww. My fucking arms hurt." This of course caught my attention, and I looked up to see a stocky young Hispanic man, perhaps in his mid-twenties, with a bushy head of black hair, holding his arms out in front of him with his hands pointing to the ceiling.

A tall, older doctor asked him, "What happened this time, Ricky?"

"I fucking fell off my board," he replied.

"You're getting too old for skateboarding, Ricky," the doctor said.

"Yeah, I know. Can you give me some fucking meds or something?"

"I'm going to check the xrays. In the meantime, I want you to sit out there so we can free this room up."

"Okay, dude, don't get all fucking grumpy."

Well, this was just the kind of entertainment I needed at that point; I texted my wife to tell her of Ricky's dilemma. As it happened, the only available seat in the row of chairs was the one directly to my right. Ricky came over and sat down, looked at me for a moment, and said, "Dude, your face is fucked up."

"Yeah, I know," I grumbled.

"Well, what happened?"

"Aww, I was at the gym, and I passed out and fell down."

"Dude, that's fucked up."

"Yeah, I know," I grumbled again.

Ricky sat quietly for a moment, then turned to me and said, "Hey, you get stoned?"

"Nahh, that's not my thing," I said.

At that moment a nurse walked by, and Ricky said, "Hey, chick! Are they gonna get me some fucking pain meds?"

She gave him an exasperated look, and said, "Just calm down, Ricky. The doctor will let you know."

"Okay, that's cool. Hey chick, you get stoned?"

This time she looked more bemused than exasperated, and said, "That was a long time ago, Ricky," and continued with her rounds.

I continued to furiously text my wife all the happenings in the emergency room chair row, when Ricky leaned out and addressed a young lady three chairs to the right. "Hey, hey chick," he said. "Why are you in here?"

As I found, the emergency room is not the place for discretion. Chick number two in Ricky's hit parade said, "Aww, I got a cyst on my ovaries."

Ricky shook his head and said, "Dude, that's fucked up. Hey, you get stoned?"

She looked at him, and with a smile said, "No, I'm cool."

At that moment, the doctor returned, took Ricky back into the examining room, and put an inflatable cast on each forearm. "Ow, that fucking hurts!" said Ricky.

When he was released to leave, Ricky walked by me and said, "Dude, I hope your face gets better."

"Me too," I said.

The moral of this story? We all need some relief, some distraction from our circumstances at times, and we must be aware enough to recognize and appreciate it when it comes. Even when it comes in the form of a loquacious, foul-mouthed, overaged stoner skateboarder named Ricky, who without question has no recollection of me, but I can say with certainty that I will never forget him.

Dude, this is the Most Awesome Day Ever!

I didn't get hurt in the following story, aside from exhaustion and extreme humiliation. You should still be able to enjoy my pain at that level, though, never fear.

As a youngster, we would occasionally visit my grandparents in their tiny house in Grover Beach, which is just directly south of Pismo Beach on the central coast area of California. I can remember walking on the pier and watching the surfers and wishing that I would be able to do that one day. My chance came many, many years later when my good friend, Miguel Wilsonian, invited me to join him for a surfing class at Pismo Beach. We had talked several times about doing this, but finally the day had come!

We cruised over from our homes in central California, and on the way I regaled Miguel with some of the stories you have read here, and he did his best to act interested, although having someone tell you their stories, at least verbally, is a little like someone telling you about the dream they had the night before. You try to be polite, but you're not really interested unless you happen to be in the dream, and then it better be flattering or there's going to be trouble. Anyway, we arrived and met the group with whom we were to share the surf class, and found that...they were all little kids, ranging from six to about ten or eleven in age. And there were about thirty of them. Two middle aged men and thirty little kids in the class.

Me: "What the hell, Wilsonian!"

Miguel: "I didn't know!"

Me: "Well what are we supposed to do, dummy?"

Miguel: "Just play along, dork!"

So, we played along. I had never worn a full wetsuit before but let me tell you they are very difficult to put on, even more difficult to take off after an exhausting day of pretending to surf and were not particularly flattering. Basically, we looked like two large seals who had swallowed pumpkins for breakfast.

All the kids got appropriately sized and weighted surfboards for their training, but Miguel and I were given these gigantic, water-logged things that seemed to exceed our body weight. The training started with jumping exercises involving lying belly down on the boards, then pushing up simultaneously with our arms and legs so as to bolt up into a standing position on the boards. This would have been somewhat difficult in gym clothes but adding the weight and resistance of a full wet suit made it resemble some kind of medieval torture strategy more than a fun activity for a Saturday morning. Of course, the little kids bounced up off their boards as if spring loaded, adding to the humiliation of the moment. My thought at the time: 'Some way, some day, I'm going to make you pay for this, Wilsonian, curse your name!'

We proceeded through several other preparatory exercises, and eventually trudged out into the surf of Pismo Beach. Just carrying the gigantic boards out to the ocean was exhausting, and we had hours to go! We gamely paddled out far enough to start attempting to ride waves, surrounded by ankle biters whose apparent sole purpose was to make us look like buffoons in comparison. Miguel had the advantage over me in that he had been surfing a number of times before, so he was somewhat more successful than me in "ridin' da waves, brah".

Most of the time I was not able to get past riding on my knees on the surfboard, which I would say was deeply embarrassing, but I was too exhausted to care at that point. I was able to get to my feet on one or two occasions, though. On one of these rare rides, one of our classmates, a loquacious little guy of about ten years old riding next to me, said "Hey, you're doing really good, man! That's cool! I'm proud of you! Isn't this great? This is the most awesome day ever! Well, see you next wave!"

"Yeah, totally awesome, dude," I grumbled. Just what I need, positive affirmations from a ten-year-old.

We struggled through to the end of the training day and faced the ordeal of taking off the full wet suit. As I writhed in the stall, attempting in vain to remove it, it crossed my mind at one point that I might just leave it on permanently, as that might be easier. I was eventually able to remove it, though, just in time for the final humiliation: the group picture. There we were, Miguel, me, and thirty little kids, the kids all with gleaming smiles, standing in front of their tiny surfboards, and Miguel and I with mammoth boards and mammoth scowls.

As we walked to the car, Miguel said, "So what do you think...want to come again next weekend?"

"I'll only do it if they have a class designed specifically for toddlers. If so, I'm in. By the way, have I told you about the Melvyns Gang?"

So, what is the moral of this story? Know your limits, guydudebro.

Just One More (Wave, That Is)

You might consider this an addendum to the last story, as they both involve a frolic in the friendly waves of the Pacific Ocean, but you would be woefully wrong. Alright, that's not true but it's my story, so I say it is.

Although classic surfing, as evidenced in the last story, is not my bag, so to speak, I have long been an avid body surfer. For those of you who have not had the pleasure, it essentially includes trundling out into the ocean until you are at least waist deep, or in my case a bit further, and wait for a good wave to break where you are. If you catch it just right, arms spread wide and legs akimbo, you can ride the top of the wave almost back to the beach. It's not as impressive to any onlookers as a gnarly ride on a surfboard, but I think it's probably equally fulfilling to the participant.

If you are familiar at all with San Diego, the wonderful (in my opinion, anyway) city near the border with Mexico, you have probably heard of Coronado Island (officially a land-tied island, but who's quibbling over that? Not me), one of the most expensive chunks of real estate in the world, and the famous Hotel Del Coronado, frequented by many a Hollywood star, rock star, political star, hell, anyone with the word star attached to them. It's quite an impressive sight, although certainly old-school in appearance; it also features a wide and glittering beach, which serves as the site for this treacherous tale. Let's go!

The weather was perfect, and the waves were bitchin', so my wife and I made the trek across the scary bridge from just south of downtown San

Diego to the island, across the quaint Coronado main street, and found our (okay, my) destination: the famous hotel and its massive beach. My wife is not inclined toward a jaunt in the waves, so she bid me good day and toddled off toward the many shops lining the main street as I strode across the sand toward what happened to be the largest waves I can ever remember in San Diego. Bigger waves are good, right? Right? Yeah, sure they are...

Since I was by myself at that point, I had left all my belongings, including, cell phone, wallet, keys, etc., in the car and agreed to meet my wife on the corner in an hour's time. I left my towel and shirt on the beach and barreled out into the dark water, experiencing that brief but brisk moment of cold ocean water meeting the nether regions, reveled at the size of the waves, and commenced my body surfing session. I had made perhaps a half-dozen rides of middling success, and honestly was a bit rattled by the magnitude of the waves. Did I mention they were large? *Here comes a particularly good one, and it's going to break right here...*

I turned to catch the monster and made one glaring error: my feet were too high. When the waves are of such proportions, having your feet above the wave may result in exactly what happened to me at that very moment: it flipped me vertical, with my head pointing directly down at the ocean floor. I didn't have time to think 'this is not good'. I was rammed, face-first, with what felt like the force of Hercules into the sandy base, and at that speed it takes on a rigidity that feels much like concrete. I saw a flash, my head twisted to the side, and... I was unconscious, just for a moment, but upside down in five feet of ocean water. Not good, broseph.

It took another moment to realize my predicament, and I righted myself, standing about shoulder deep at that point, when a thought crossed my mind: I think my neck might be broken. Yikes. This relaxing, enjoyable trip is getting worse by the second. *Okay, take a deep breath... rotate your neck... hurts but if it was broken, I don't think I'd be standing in the water, I'd probably be at the ocean floor commiserating with Davy Jones in his locker or Captain Hook or some other dead pirate...*

Next, I realized the right side of my face was burning. Smashing into the ocean floor face first will apparently do that to you. Then, there was the whole momentarily unconscious thing... I trudged toward the beach, but... okay, my neck's not broken, my face is burning, and I feel a little dizzy, but... I mean, I don't feel *that* bad...

Yes, you guessed it, I turned and caught two or three more waves before feeling too nauseous to continue. This time I made it to the beach, feeling intensely woozy, located my towel, wrapped it around my shoulders, and stumbled toward the ritzy hotel, thinking I needed to find a bathroom so that I could check my still burning face. Hotel Coronado features an underground shopping area, and I remembered seeing public bathrooms down there from a previous visit. I made my way through the area, drawing looks of either concern or disgust, it was hard to tell which, from the mostly wealthy patrons. And who could blame them; when I finally did locate the bathroom and peered into the mirror, the person looking back only tangentially resembled me. The right side of my face was skinned and beet red, I had a sand-covered towel draped over my shoulders, no shirt, gym shorts, and torn flip flops on. I'm sure the folks in the hotel thought that a homeless fellow must have bumbled onto the property, but honestly, I was too dizzy and out of it to care at that point. The *coup de grâce:* I found a clock which told me I had only been out there for twenty minutes and had another forty minutes to wait before meeting with my wife, who had the keys to the car, wherein my phone and wallet were currently residing. *Oh, crap.*

I plodded out to the street, heedless of the stares and parents shepherding their children away from me, and considered attempting to find her, but honestly, I don't think I could have walked much further. So, I sat on a bus stop bench, and eventually reclined on the bench. When at long last my wife stumbled upon me, she was equal parts concerned and amused, which was certainly understandable.

Will I ever body surf again? After all you've read if you've made it this far, is that even a question? *I might be riding the waves right now, as far as you know...*

Well, friends, I think that's enough for now. I have many more tales to tell, though, so stay tuned. If you would be so kind, please consider submitting a review; as an author, your feedback is especially important to me. Just go to your book retailer of choice, type in my name, and you know what to do from there. Thank you!

And, as a special bonus for those who have made it this far, please find below a short story entitled, Always Read the Fine Print. Enjoy!

Always Read the Fine Print

A short story, written to the prompt: Release The Kraken!

"RE-E-E-E-LEASE THE crack, Ken!" she bleated; of course, being half goat causes you to sound that way naturally. Ken, from his immense, ornate granite throne, waved his arms in a bizarre, synchronized pattern, his cryptid brow furrowed in concentration.

"Arrr! Rarrr!" he cried, momentarily forgetting that Pansy, an unfortunate but descriptive name for such a timid creature, did not understand the Bigfoot vernacular. "Oh, sorry, P, but holding the sky together takes a lot of attention. Why would I want to release it?"

"Wha-a-a-a-a-a-t, not this aga-a-a-a-in. I've told you a mi-i-i-lion times, the rest of my band is on the other si-i-i-ide," she replied, her horns fairly shaking with frustration.

"Now listen, P, as you well know, keeping this crack in the sky from expanding and swallowing up reality takes all my mental energy. I don't have any space left to remember things like that. What is it you play again? The pan flute?" the great, hairy beast grunted, straining at his burden.

She hopped with exasperation, her hooves clicking like stilettos on travertine. "I don't find your stereo-o-o-o-typing humorous, Ken. You know I play guitar, a sixty-seven telecaster to be exa-a-a-a-a-a-ct."

"See, that's exactly why I can't let it go. A sixty-seven telecaster won't be invented for another two thousand years. I can't let you and your hippie friends go traipsing through time again."

"You're pretty ju-u-u-u-u-dgemental for a giant imaginary monster, you know tha-a-a-a-t? They are no-o-o-o-o-t hippies. They just like to have fu-u-u-u-n. We have a gig for the dead coming u-u-u-u-p, and we need to rehearse. Co-o-o-o-o-me on, Ken!"

"Obviously you're mistaken about the imaginary part, and you mean to tell me you're doing a gig with the Grateful Dead?"

"No-o-o-o-o, not with the Dead, for the de-e-e-e-e-ad. We're setting up next to the ri-i-i-i-ver Styx. It's going to be e-e-e-e-epic."

"Wait a minute, you're playing with Styx? Is it the original lineup?"

"You're impo-o-o-o-sible, Ken. And who knew you were such a connisu-u-u-u-er of classic rock? How long have you been ho-o-o-o-lding that crack together, anywa-a-a-a-y?"

"Let's see... what time is it?"

"Almost noo-o-o-o-o-n."

"Seven hundred years, thirteen days, and four hours, minus bathroom breaks."

As they spoke, the rift in the sky undulated wildly, the crimson fires beyond the fracture clearly visible against the infinite cerulean backdrop.

"How'd you get stuck with this du-u-u-u-ty, anyway?" queried Pansy, seating herself on the arm of the granite throne and crossing her coarsely furred legs, hooves dangling suggestively.

"Don't try to get flirty with me, little missy. That's how I got in this spot in the first place, you know. As it turned out, I was irresistible to the demigods of both sexes, and the boss gods got a bit jealous. Knowing my altruistic nature, they set me to this task, assuming that I wouldn't refuse it and let reality be destroyed, like some people I know probably would, and that it would take all my attention, meaning I would no longer have time to, oh, let's say, *entertain* the demigods, if you know what I mean."

"No, tell me wha-a-a-a-at you mean," she murmured, batting her eyelashes and twirling her delicately braided goatee.

"Oh, come on, P, don't play with my emotions. I can't let your band come through, and you know it. But now I'm a little curious, and I need something to take my mind off these rotator cuff injuries I have from holding my arms up like this for seven hundred years. Tell me about your other band members. Maybe there's some other way I can help out."

Pansy's eyes lit up, the vertical pupils shining in the afternoon sun. "Oh, we have quite a li-i-i-i-neup. My cousin, Cupid, is playing the harp, and he wa-a-a-a-ails, let me tell you. He's a mischievous little devil, too; keeps things interesting on the to-o-o-o-o-o-ur bus, that's for sure."

"You mean Cupid, the naked baby with the bow? I could have used him and his lead arrows; that might have kept me out of this mess in the first place. Who else you got?"

"Let's see... we have Briares on the drums. You should see-e-e-e-e that dude jam. He plays like he has a hu-u-u-u-undred hands. Well, he does have a hu-u-u-undred hands, but still."

"Oh, I think I've met him. Tall and ugly, can't keep his hundred hands to himself?"

"Ha-a-a-a-a! I guess you ha-a-a-ve met him. Then there's Cyclops, everyone knows hi-i-i-i-m. Kinda quiet, likes to ha-a-a-ang back, but don't get him ma-a-a-a-d. He plays bass, of co-o-o-ourse."

Still grunting, but now out of excitement, Ken said, "Wait, you got ol' Cycie? He's a legend! If you have him, I know you're playing some funk."

"Oh, yeah, bro, it's downright sta-a-a-anky. Did I tell you about my ho-o-o-orn section? All centaurs, and you should see them da-a-a-ance when they're not playing. They're the most so-o-o-oulful half-horses you ever saw. Hey, you know wha-a-a-t? I see what all those de-e-e-emigods were attracted to. You're cu-u-u-u-te."

"I told you, don't tempt me, girl. I have a job to do, and I will not be deterred. Now look, I can't let them in, regardless of how flashy their licks are. The best I can do is let you go over there. If I opened it up wide enough for those giants to come through, a bunch of this reality would get sucked over to that side, time would stop working properly, the boss gods would get royally pissed, and no one needs that, especially me."

"Oh, all right," she brayed petulantly, dropping with a *clop!* from the arm of the great throne. "Ho-o-o-w am I supposed to get o-o-o-o-ver there? This would sure be a whole lot ea-a-a-sier if you would just do what I asked and release the cra-a-a-a-ck, Ken. By the way, I've been wo-o-o-ndering. How did you get involved with the Gre-e-e-eks? I mean, o-o-o-o-bviously you're not from around here, and rapid transit has not been inve-e-e-e-ented yet, plus as far as I know, Bigfoots, Yetis, Sasquatches, wha-a-atever you are, ca-a-a-a-n't speak. Everyone knows the-e-e-e-re are Minotaurs, and Harpies, and lots of other wei-i-i-i-i-rd combo-creatures like me, but a talking Yowie? That's cra-a-a-a-a-zy."

As he continued to make his strange, parallel arm movements, Ken roared, "Oh, now who's doing the stereotyping? In fact, that's not just stereotyping, that's racist. Or is that species-ist? I'm not sure, but either way, not cool. I have a good mind not to help you out at all."

"Aww, co-o-o-o-me on, Ken, I didn't mean it tha-a-a-a-at way. You're blowing this wa-a-a-a-ay out of proportion."

"Oh, now I'm over-reacting, huh? The poor, primitive creature can't control his emotions, is that what you're saying? You know what is sad about this? You're so much a product of your milieu, you don't even know what you said is wrong, and especially not why. You have never lived my experience, so you could never know my pain. Oh, Lord, I wish I had a gospel choir to back me up right now; I would get my preach on for real, then."

"Ken, you just u-u-u-u-sed the word milieu. I think you-u-u-u-u made your point. I'm so-o-o-o-o-rry, I'll try to be better."

"Oh, I guess I did. Look, the truth is, I didn't really have the right physical equipment for speaking, one of the boss gods gifted me with that. I was always smart, though. I just couldn't talk because I didn't have the hook-up."

"Well, we all ha-a-a-a-ave our struggles. You speak pe-e-e-erfectly now, and I sound like a g-o-o-o-at who speaks Greek."

The monstrous cryptid flinched and grimaced mightily; he felt the demonic presences on the other side of the gap looking for ways to gain purchase and scramble through as they so frequently tried, and he was reminded, through his struggle, that he remained the only line of defense against chaos and destruction. He also knew that it was getting close to the end of the shift on the other side, and he would have a little reprieve as the demonic hordes punched out and the next group punched in. They always took a little time for chit-chat, and this was the time he took his bathroom breaks. He knew from seven-hundred years of experience that one of the few things the devilish entities respected was the need for that delicious sense of bowel and intestinal void.

"Listen, P, I gotta go take care of business. When I get back, we'll work on getting you over to your band, okay?"

She jumped and clapped, thrilled at the prospect of finally getting back together with her mythical, musical mates. She went into a little jig, the clacking of her hooves echoing off the face of the sheer stone cliff behind Ken's throne. As she spun, she gazed at the sun reflecting off the waves of the Mediterranean, like a million-million Bic lighters celebrating her dance skills. Of course, Bic lighters would also not be invented for another two thousand years, but she had been around the block a few times and had seen some things.

She was startled from her reverie by Ken, reappearing with none other than Pegasus, the winged horse. "Hey, P, look who I rounded up. Your problem is solved. 'Ol Pegsie can get you up there in no time, then just jump through the gap; you half-goats are good at that, right?"

"At what, jumping through ga-a-a-a-ps?"

"Okay, that sounded nasty, but you know what I meant. And what I think you meant to say was, 'Oh, thank you, Ken, I don't know how I'll ever repay you,' right?"

"Of co-o-o-ourse that's what I meant, cu-u-utie."

"Oh, one last thing, P. I need you to sign this form, it's just a release of liability. I don't want to get sued if you fall off Pegsie or get burned by eternal hellfire or whatnot. Just gotta cover the old backside, you know what I mean."

She stared at the paper for a moment, and said, "I can't read all of thi-i-i-i-s, I have ADHD. It all looks Gree-e-e-k to me."

"Well, maybe that's because it's written in Greek. Just sign it, Pegsie is getting anxious."

After a few strokes of Ken's quill, the document was signed. "Hey, did I ever tell you I play guitar too?" Ken asked, resting his elbow on his knee and placing his fist under his chin.

"No-o-o-o-o. That's cool. Well, time to get go-o-o-o-o-ing."

"Hang on a minute. Does your band play the blues?"

"Sure, twelve-bar, shuffles, Chica-a-a-a-a-go, we can do it a-a-a-a-ll. I gotta go, Ke-e-e-e-en."

"Yeah, you know, it's hard for me to play guitar with these fat Bigfoot fingers, so I just play slide, tune to an open key. I figure if it's okay for Bonnie Raitt, it's okay for me."

"Wait, don't tell me you know Bonnie Ra-a-a-a-a-itt."

"Well, I know of her. See, I spent a lot of time over on that side of the crack, too. Been all up and down the timeline, played all over. Oh, by the way, you fell for the second-oldest trick in the book. Gotta read the fine print, P."

As the crack between worlds undulated threateningly, Ken rose, placed both hairy hands on Pansy's shoulders, and said, "Due to your agreement, via binding signature, to accept the power that was given to me to maintain the integrity of the rift, I hereby transfer all power, and resultant responsibility, to you, Miss Pansy, in perpetuity, or until such time as you are able to find a suitable replacement. I release the crack to you, and I and the boss gods thank you for accepting this burden. Okay, well, enough with the legalities. Go on, have seat, the throne is now yours."

Pansy stomped her hooves, and shouted, "No-o-o-o-t fair, Ken! You tri-i-i-i-cked me!"

Ken smiled sympathetically. "Sorry, P, but you tricked yourself. Do a good job, now; it's no fun to be smote by the boss gods, believe me. Or is it smited? Either way, it's a bummer. You ready, Pegsie?"

The regal horse unfurled its massive wings as Ken reached behind the granite throne. A moment later, he was on Pegasus' back, holding... a sixty-seven telecaster. "I just happened to have one of these too, P. I'll tell the fellas hello for you, and the guys in Styx as well. 'Bye!"

Waving her arms angrily from her perch on the throne, she cried, "It's the ri-i-i-i-ver Styx, not the band, you stu-u-u-u-u-pid Skunk Ape!" But it was too late, Ken was already beyond the crack, and the faint sounds of jamming and laughter could not compete with the anguished bleating filling the air.

More Bonus Content: Singular

Prologue

NEW YEAR'S EVE, 2051. It was either the beginning or the end depending on how you look at it, but to me, in a literal way, it was both.

We were late, speeding through the stormy streets of Riverside, California. It had been the kind of gray day that can make you feel dull and strip you of motivation, but not for us. We were on our way to meet dad for our three-person New Year's Eve party: just mom, dad, and me. That's how it had been since... well, long as I could remember, all my nine years. As we rolled through the warm rain, mom told me that years ago, before the Great Pacific Tsunami of 2036, it hardly ever rained in Southern California, but all that had changed. It now rained often, although it was generally hot enough that the rain quickly evaporated, keeping everything perpetually moist and uncomfortable with humidity.

I remember thinking, as my mom spoke, how pretty she seemed. Very petite, with soft features and sensibly short auburn hair; she was not the kind of person to spend a lot of time fussing with her appearance. The whole thing was topped off by over-large black horn-rimmed glasses, which just seemed right on her. "See, there was lots of disagreement back in those days over global warming, but after the Tsunami, well, that pretty much ended the disagreements, although even after that disaster, there are still some people who deny. Hard to understand... anyway, almost all the polar ice had melted, and the sea level was rising each year, and finally the extra weight of the water triggered a cascade of undersea earthquakes in the Pacific Ocean. It was way before you were born, but there used to be land and millions and millions of people 20 miles further out from where the coast is now, but the tsunami wiped it all out."

"Mom, what's a cascade?"

Mom laughed, and said, "That's the question you have after all that? You're funny, buddy boy."

I didn't really understand what was so funny, but I kept quiet, so mom would keep going. I loved hearing her talk, even though I didn't understand everything. "Anyway, all the coastal areas of the Pacific Ocean were completely decimated, and a lot of land is now under water. There used to be a very powerful country called Japan, but except for some mountain areas it's all under water, along with most of the Philippines, the Hawaiian Islands, all the Pacific rim countries, and more than... well, let's just say lots and lots of people too."

A kid from a normal family would probably be wondering why his mom would be telling him such a horrible story, but I was quite used to it, even as a nine-year-old. To say my parents were nerds would be... well, nerds think of my parents as nerds. My mom had a Ph.D in Astrophysics and seemed to know everything, and wanted to make sure I got exposed to as much as I could handle, especially things she found important or interesting, which was quite a lot, by the way. My dad, a Ph.D in Conceptual Physics and Nano-Engineering, was working on a project that he couldn't talk about, which of course made mom and me crazy.

Anyway, we continued down the dark, wet streets toward dad's office, and as we reached the freeway, mom took her hands off the wheel and allowed the mag-strips in the asphalt to steer and propel the car. She explained that some of the newer freeways had the mag strips, but most didn't have them yet, and probably never would. She programmed the car to take the correct turn-off, turned to me and continued her story. "Take out your phone and check for video of the tsunami. You'll be amazed. We were lucky, dad and me, that we were able to get out in time and get up here into the hills. We probably would have..."

The car swerved quickly to the right, then auto-corrected its course, throwing both of us from side to side. "*Whoa*, that was close. Crazy petrol-heads! I know things are hard, but why anyone would still drive those old junkers is a mystery to me, and that guy was all over the road, like he was racing or something. Anyway, as I was saying..." There was a sudden screeching sound, and somehow, I felt like I was doing summersaults, over and over... And that was the last time I heard my mom's voice. In fact, it was the last time I heard anything for quite a while.

1

The lights are very bright; I blink furiously but can't seem to get my eyes to clear. Lots of people around; don't recognize most of them, but my dad is here. They're all standing over me; I don't understand why they are all looking at me in this way. Then I notice that some of them are wearing the "scrubs" that nurses and doctors wear; am I in the hospital or something? Through my blurry, unfocused eyes dad looks exhausted with worry. What's going on here? Did I get hurt or something? And where's mom? My throat doesn't seem to work, and I can't make any words come out; it sounds strange to my ears, like dull grunting and squeaking. That's weird...did I get my tonsils out or something? I can't remember anything about getting sick or...

Then, in a flash, it all came back to me. Driving along, chatting happily with mom, then an ear-shattering sound, flipping over and over and then... nothing. All the people assembled around me have deeply concerned expressions. I try to feel my body by moving different extremities, but I am not having much luck; nothing seems to be happening. Fear creeps into my mind, but dad's face is suddenly hovering close. "Luke, Lukey, can you hear me? It's me, dad."

I looked at dad like he was crazy, and tried to say, "Of course I can hear you,", but again only grunts came out. *This is frustrating! What the heck is going on here?*

Although he was always kind of wiry, dad looked positively bony, and his dark hair was much longer and messy, like he hadn't been taking care of himself. His ocean blue eyes, which I had always thought were his best feature, were now clouded. All in all, he looked as if he was being squeezed from all sides by tremendous pressure. *How could his hair be longer? I just saw him yesterday! Would somebody please tell me what is going on?*

Dad looked deeply into my eyes, and although he was smiling, he seemed sad at the same time, which I thought was weird. "Lukey, you can hear me, can't you? I can see it in your face. I didn't think this day would ever come." Then a big tear rolled down his cheek, landing on the bed covers just below my chin. I had never seen my dad cry before, and it made me want to cry too. *What is wrong? What's going on with everyone? I don't get it...*

A deep, gruff voice from behind dad called out. "Dr. Taylor, I'm sorry to interrupt, but I need to speak with you. This is very important."

Dad turned and slowly crossed the room to where the man with the long white coat was standing. He seemed to think that I couldn't hear or understand him, but I could. "I'm very sorry, Dr. Taylor, but we need to discuss what to do here. We have been keeping your son alive for quite a long time at your request and considerable cost, and it is clear there is no hope of any kind of recovery. You can see that. I know this is difficult but keeping him alive this way is not good for him or you. There's nothing left, and we don't have the technology to change it. I mean, no arms, no legs, half a torso gone, an artificial heart, there is nothing more we can do. It's been five years, and it is time to move on. I know you can see that. Yes, there is some brain activity, but if we remove the life support, he would go quickly."

As the man in the long white coat spoke, dad hung his head and rubbed his hands across his face. Following a long pause, he said, "Look, I know you mean well, Dr. Torres. I do, and I'm not a fool. I just need a little more time to accept it. Give me until tomorrow morning, please. Then I'll be ready."

He turned his face up to the man in the white coat who I now knew as Dr. Torres, and he had big tears in his eyes. *Wait... did he say I don't have any legs or arms anymore?*

Dr. Torres let out a big sigh, and said, "Of course, tomorrow would be fine. It's really for the best, Dr. Taylor, although I understand how difficult this is. I'm very sorry." He looked at dad for a moment, glanced over at me, turned and briskly exited the room, the other staff members following him.

Dad glanced up at the clock on the wall, strode over to me, and knelt beside the bed. "Don't worry, Lukey. I know you can hear me. Everything will be all right, you'll see. I'll be back tonight. In the meantime, just rest. I love you, Lukey, I won't let them take you. I promise." He had tears in his eyes again, and I still didn't quite understand what was happening. He leaned forward, kissed me on the forehead, and bolted from the room.

He said I don't have any arms or legs, but... that can't be true, can it? What happened to them? I wish I could see better... I almost feel like I can only open one eye, and the one I can open won't focus right... Suddenly I felt exhausted, and I guess I fell asleep.

"Luke... Lukey, wake up, It's me, dad. Listen carefully. I'm going to do some things that I'll explain later, and then we're going to get out of here. Some of this may hurt a little bit, but stay as quiet as you can, ok?"

I tried to answer but only a little squeak came out. I glanced at the clock on the wall: eleven-fifteen p.m. Dad put a chair up against the door to block it so that it could not be opened and rolled two large metallic suitcases to the side of the bed. Actually, I'm not sure they were suitcases; they were about the right size, but were square and plain, and emitted a faint buzz. He opened one of them, and in it was a large glass cylinder, maybe half a meter tall and wide, filled with some weird material about the color of my skin. I stared, transfixed by the movement of the stuff in the cylinder. Not like it was fluid, but more like it was *alive.* There were some wires hooked to the top of the cylinder; dad disconnected the wires and hoisted the cylinder up, setting it next to me on the bed, and it must have been heavy because he really had to struggle to lift it. He pulled back my covers, and let out a gasp, more tears spilling from his eyes. He picked up the container with the weird stuff in it and poured it onto the bed where my body would be, and right away I could feel it sort of connecting to me, worming its way into what was left of my flesh and bones, and it all seemed to happen very quickly, like the weird material knew just what to do. *That feels strange... wait, I haven't felt anything in a long time down there... what is happening? Oww, that hurts... my foot hurts... hold on, I thought I didn't have any feet...*

Dad bent over, opened the other suitcase, and in it was another glass container of the stuff. He picked this one up, again with what appeared to be great difficulty, and poured it on my head and upper body. I felt it mixing with my skin, and forming itself into... *wait, that hurts, but... my eye... I can see out of both eyes now...*

"Dad, I can see again!" *Did I just talk out loud? How did that happen?*

Dad fumbled with something else in the second suitcase, came up with an object about the size of a marble, and pushed it into the material that was attaching itself to the side of my head. He bent over again, produced another item about the size and shape of a baseball, and worked it into the material that was melding to the middle of my body. He tapped for a minute on a tablet computer, and I could feel the baseball-sized thing vibrating slightly. After some more tapping... well, this is hard to describe. Or, maybe not hard, but totally unexpected. I heard a woman's voice in my head; not like someone was talking to me, but like someone else was thinking words and I could hear them in my mind.

"Stand by, initiating boot procedure," she said.

My eyes bulged out and I thrashed around; dad came in close and whispered, "Try to hold still just a little longer, Lukey. We're almost ready to get out of here. I'll explain everything soon, but we have to get moving right away."

Dad seemed anxious, almost panicked, as he waited for whatever was happening to me to finish, when suddenly... an aggressive pounding at the door.

2

"Okay, here we go... Lukey, don't ask any questions or say anything, just do as I say, and we'll get out of here safely, okay?"

I nodded, fear increasing with each moment that passed. "Sorry, ah, just a moment please," dad shouted through the door. He thrust back into one of the cases and pulled out... a long blonde wig, a black hoodie sweatshirt, a powder blue t-shirt, some hot pink shorts, and flip-flops with rhinestones. "Okay, quickly now, Lukey, let's get you up."

He helped me to a sitting position, and I felt wobbly and out of control. "This is going to feel weird for a few minutes, but just concentrate on moving your body normally. You'll have to think about it for a bit, but eventually it will work automatically, just like normal," dad hissed in my ear. He was right, too... I had to think about moving my arms before they would move, and the same for my legs. It was difficult, and I had to give it all my concentration. My legs and arms looked mostly normal, but they were much larger than I remembered, almost as if I had aged five years overnight.

As I worked on getting my body to move, I took a good look at dad. His hair was combed carefully, unlike the last time I saw him, although it was still too long and looked unwashed. Worry still painted his face, and he must have just shaved for the first time in a while, as he had a couple of nicks on the side of his chin. He was wearing a blue shirt that seemed almost military in style... in fact all his clothes gave that impression, as if he dressed anticipating action. I found that very strange, as I had never seen him dress even remotely that way before; in fact, he often wore shorts and tennis shoes.

There was insistent pounding at the door, and someone shouted, "Please open the door immediately, Dr. Taylor."

"Yes, yes, I'll be right there. My niece and I are just saying our last goodbyes, you understand."

I looked around, thinking maybe I missed the other person in the room, but dad made eye contact with me and whispered, "Okay, Lukey, let's get these clothes and wig on you, quick."

"Oh, I get it," I mouthed in return. "I'm supposed to be the niece, and you're sneaking me out of here! Kind of like you're busting me out of jail or something, right?"

"Dad offered a quick smile, and said, "That's exactly right. Now just keep your head down and pretend you're crying, okay? We have to put on a good show, otherwise we might get caught."

I was still a little scared, but it also seemed exciting. Dad put the clothes and wig on me and put the hood up over my head. "Now look down as we leave, and don't say anything. If we're lucky, we may get out of here yet."

"Wait, what do you mean if we're lucky?"

"Sorry, Lukey, no more questions right now. We have to go."

Dad rolled the two cases into the corner of the room next to the window and pressed a button on the back of each of them. "All right, here we go. Just concentrate on moving as normally as you can. It's going to feel strange, like I said, but you're smart, you'll figure it out."

I stood up, which took all my concentration, and I felt like I was falling forward, and then realized that I was. Suddenly, it was like one of those inflatable toys that you can't knock over, or maybe more like there was a gyroscope in my body keeping me from falling, because my body just came back up to standing on its own. *Wow, that was weird... this whole thing is... unbelievable, that's what it is...*

Dad grabbed me by the hand, which, strangely enough, felt like someone grabbing me by the hand, and I caught a glimpse of myself in the mirror as we walked to the door. *Man, I got tall all of a sudden... can't really see my face through this wig and hoodie, though...* I had to put all my mental energy into getting my legs and arms to move, but I could feel it getting easier with each step, as if they were learning how to move on their own. As he reached to move the chair away from the door, I said, Dad, what..."

"Shhh, not now, Lukey," he hissed, and pulled the door open. There were three big men in black suits at the door, along with Dr. Torres. "My apologies, gentlemen, my niece and I had to make one last visit before... well, you understand."

Dr. Torres and the men all wore stern expressions. "Yes, of course, but I'm afraid these men have some questions for you, Dr. Taylor. If you'll just walk this way."

Oh no, that doesn't sound good... I looked at dad, and I thought it strange that he appeared to be counting under his breath. There was a loud *pop!* from the far corner of the room where dad had left the cases; flames leapt out of them, and Dr. Torres and the three men rushed into the room, shouting and frantically looking for the fire extinguisher. Dad grabbed my hand again and we hustled down the hall; when we reached the end, we went through a large metal door that said "Stairs" on it. Once inside we sprinted down the gray metal stairwell, which was harshly lit by uncovered overhead florescent bulbs. Moving quickly was almost impossible for me at first, but after a few steps it was as if my body got the idea and started moving fast. I mean, *really* fast. I passed dad up and was at the bottom of three flights of stairs before he was halfway down. *How did that happen?* Dad called down to me, "Hold it there, we need to make sure no one is waiting for us on the other side of the door before we go out. I'm sorry, Lukey, but we're in a little bit of trouble and we need to be extra cautious."

"But dad, why..."

"I'll explain everything when we're safe, I promise." Dad had reached the bottom of the stairs, breathing heavily, his face covered in sweat. He opened the heavy steel door just a crack, put his eye up to the gap, and after a moment said, "I think the coast is clear. The diversion I set seems to have pulled everyone from their security up to the third floor, so I think we are good to go. Take your hoodie off and just act like it's a normal day; we don't want to draw any attention to ourselves if we can help it." I took the sweatshirt off and hadn't noticed that the shirt dad put on me had a white unicorn on it, with a rainbow coming out of the cartoon unicorn's horn. "Dad, don't you think you went a little overboard with the girl clothes?"

"Not now, Lukey... okay, yes, maybe I did. Quiet now, act normal." He pulled on a black cap with an orange "SF" on the front, put on some sunglasses, and we strolled out of the stairwell as if we were taking a walk through the park.

Dad took my hand, and we sauntered toward the front of the hospital, while fire alarms blared from everywhere. As we approached the main entrance, I noticed people sitting on the floor and on every seat, dozens of them, and most of them appeared... well, they were dirty, like they had been sleeping outdoors, and many had backpacks or other bags or sacks with them. Most appeared alone, but there were some whole families as well.

"Dad, what are all these people doing here?" I whispered, not wanting to insult anyone.

He looked down for a moment, a pained expression clouding his face. "I'm sorry, Lukey, your... your mom and I tried to shelter you from the problems of the world, but it was like this before... before the accident, and it's gotten progressively worse over the past five years. I'll explain it all if we are able to get out of here without getting stopped," he murmured in reply.

We were about thirty meters from the entrance, and as if right on cue, I noticed a tall man with a black suit and sunglasses just inside the sliding glass doors. He clearly saw us as well and was watching with great interest while talking quickly into his wrist. Dad steered me hurriedly through a door to the right into what appeared to be an office of some kind. The man in the suit was moving in our direction as we entered the office, but before he reached us dad again barred the door with a chair. The office was empty and dark, and it occurred to me that the hospital staff had probably evacuated because of the fire alarm that continued blasting its high-pitched wail. There was a deep *whump!* on the office door. I glanced at the clock on the wall: it was now just after midnight.

"Okay, Lukey, we have to find a way out of here... let's see if there is a window or door to the outside anywhere..." We dashed around the front of the office but there was no way out, so we went back into the room at the rear, behind a counter and swinging half-door.

"Dad, why is that man after us? Why are we trying to get away from him?"

Before he had a chance to reply, I noticed a restroom behind the second room, and ran in; there, in the back of the restroom, above the toilet, was a small window. "Lukey, do you think you can get through there?" dad asked, an edge of panic in his voice.

"I think so, but how about you?"

"Oh, I'll get through, don't worry. Ready?"

Without waiting for an answer, dad grabbed a large stapler from one of the desks and smashed it against the window. On the third blow, the window shattered, and his hand was sliced by a piece of falling glass, blood splattering the toilet. He grimaced in pain and grunted, "All right, Lukey, here we go..." He lifted me up to the high window and pushed me through. I felt chunks of glass slicing through my new body, but it didn't hurt, and it didn't hurt when I landed on my backside on the concrete sidewalk outside the window either. I looked at my hands and arms; no cuts, no blood, nothing. *Now that's weird... dad better explain what's going on quick or I'm going to explode from curiosity... and why hasn't that voice in my head said anything else?*

Dad tumbled out the window, shouting "Run! To the left, toward the park across the street... Hand me your hoodie, I have to wrap up my hand, so I don't leave a trail of blood for them to follow. Go!"

We sprinted across the street, and in the background the man in the suit was shouting at us to stop; he had made his way into the office but was too big to get through the window. Suddenly I heard a loud pop, and something struck me hard in the back; it knocked me forward, but again whatever was in me that was balancing me kept me from falling over, and I continued to run. Within moments we were out of sight of the window, and dad was speaking frantically into his earpiece microphone. We were running through the heavily forested park when a small black car careened across the grass, skidding to a stop in front of us. The rear door flew open, and dad screamed, "Get in!"

We dove into the rear seat as the car sped off, tumbling us about as it twisted around trees and then out of the far side of the park and onto the freeway. "Dad, this is like some kind of crazy movie or something! What's happening?"

"We've got to get away, Lukey, but I have a plan. Hang on! Thanks for the quick pick up, Minh, now to drop-off one!"

The lady in the driver's seat held up her right thumb in response and sped down the freeway at what felt like a high rate. "Lukey, this is one of my associates, Minh Houng. She helped me with some of the... technology issues, let's call them."

I managed a glance at Ms. Houng as we careened down the freeway, and she was sneaking peeks at me in the rearview mirror every chance she got as well. She had stalk-straight, jet black hair, almost cartoonishly messy, and appeared tall and very slim, although it was hard to tell for sure while being thrown from side to side in the backseat. "So, John, all is working?" she asked in heavily accented English.

Dad turned to me, grinning mildly, and said, "Yes... yes, I think we did good. Thank you, Minh, I couldn't have done it without you."

"Well, is not over yet, so hold on, here is exit..."

We flew off the freeway, took a quick turn and came to a skidding stop under an overpass. Another small car was stopped directly in front of us, this one a faded tan color; dad grabbed my hand, and we bolted from the black car and tumbled into the rear seat of the tan car. The driver peeled out and flew down the road before we had even closed the door. I looked back at the small black car, and Ms. Houng was pulling off a coating from her car to reveal that it was actually white. *Wow, that was smart... they had this whole thing planned...*

Our new car made several quick turns down neighborhood streets before slowing to a normal pace. "Keep your heads down and hang on to your knickers, mates, I reckon I'll have you dags clear soon. That was some hard yakka, but you made it, eh? Good on ya!" said the man driving, as he slapped his thigh in delight.

He had a huge bush of black hair, dark brown skin, and was startlingly thin. He also had a strange accent I wasn't familiar with, and appeared to be about dad's age, although it was hard to tell for sure. He was wearing worn out cargo shorts, tall work boots, and a short-sleeved, army green shirt with the name "Pedro" embroidered on the left front pocket. "Dad, what did he say?" I whispered, not wanting to take the chance of insulting our driver.

Dad chuckled, and then the driver started chuckling, and within a few moments they were both laughing like madmen. I thought it was all unbearably strange, and I needed some answers. When he was finally calm enough to speak, dad said, "Lukey, say hello to Dr. Benji Walker. He's a bit hard to understand for you because he's from Australia. He's an aboriginal. One of the few aboriginal scientists. He built your main power source."

"My... my what?"

Dad chuckled again. "Oh, there's so much to tell you, Lukey. Just hang tight, as soon as we get to the lab, I'll explain everything."

Dr. Walker was watching me excitedly in the rearview mirror, his black eyes shining and his wide, flat nose flaring wildly. "Crikey, John, it really worked, eh? What a beauty! Everything's on line, no worries?"

Dad turned to me, smiling through tears. "Yes, I think so. Against all odds, here is my boy."

Other Books By Larry Buenafe

About the Author

LARRY BUENAFE HAS BEEN writing seriously for several years; before that, he was writing in a frivolous and immature manner. He is an avid reader of science and science fiction of all kinds. He has seven other books currently available, probably at your favorite book retailer, including, in the Ferdie and The Seven series, **When the Angels are Gone**, **Time *Flies,*** and **Fractals,** and in the Singular science fiction series, **Singular**, **Forever, Reboot, and Reassemble**. In the real world, he is a recently retired high school administrator (there are some unwritten books contained in those experiences, I can assure you) and part-time musician. Would he make his living via writing if he could? Why yes, yes, he would. Perhaps you could help with that endeavor. He lives in central California with his wonderful wife and has two amazing daughters. Wonderful? Amazing? Yes, he insists it is so.

Connect with Larry Buenafe

FACEBOOK: Larry Buenafe Author[1]

Goodreads: Larry Buenafe Author Profile[2]

Instagram: larry buenafe author instagram[3]

1. https://www.facebook.com/FerdieandtheSeven/
2. https://www.goodreads.com/author/show/16421536.Larry_Buenafe
3. https://www.instagram.com/larrybuenafeauthor/

www.ingramcontent.com/pod-product-compliance
Lightning Source LLC
LaVergne TN
LVHW090049160826
845672LV00015B/1611

9798230035985